A Geographia Guide

Hants & Dorset

Bournemouth, New Forest,
Coast and Countryside

INCLUDING

CHRISTCHURCH
POOLE
SWANAGE
CORFE CASTLE
LULWORTH COVE
WEYMOUTH
DORCHESTER
LYME REGIS
SHAFTESBURY
SHERBORNE
SALISBURY
BEAULIEU
SOUTHAMPTON
PORTSMOUTH & SOUTHSEA
HAYLING ISLAND
WINCHESTER

 Geographia Ltd
63 Fleet Street
London, EC4Y 1PE

Guide to Hants & Dorset
ISBN 0 09 205400 5
© Geographia Ltd.,
63 Fleet Street,
London, EC4Y IPE

Compiled and published by
Geographia Ltd.

Contributors: E. L. Coster, Gavin Gibbons and G. Grove

Photographic illustrations
British Tourist Authority

Line illustrations: G. Cowan

Series Editor: J. T. Wright

Made and printed in Great Britain by
The Anchor Press Ltd.,
Tiptree, Essex

Contents

Illustrations

THE COUNTRYSIDE DESCRIBED IN THIS GUIDE is that of central, southern England. The whole comprises a delightfully varied area ranging from the chalk uplands of north and east Hampshire to the forest glades and rich vegetation of the New Forest in the south-west of that county, and including the rolling chalk downs and beautiful valleys of Dorset and the Wiltshire fringe.

Within these boundaries there are high view-points in abundance, fine old country houses, many a castle ruin, abbeys, churches and old inns, as well as the attractive, ancient cathedral cities of Winchester and Salisbury, where it is still possible to enjoy the tranquillity of green closes and handsome lawns.

Vivid Contrasts

In contrast there is the transatlantic port of Southampton and, of course, the many pleasant seaside resorts catering for the tastes and needs of a great variety of holidaymakers. There is Bournemouth with its mild climate, serene atmosphere and traffic-free promenades; Swanage with its safe, sandy beaches on the north side of its bay; Weymouth, still retaining a little of its Georgian charm, and Lyme Regis with its historic stone Cobb, and air of gentle dignity which made it fashionable as long ago as the eighteenth century. Indeed, this sweep of the English Channel coast offers wide-ranging interest, peace and tranquillity, as well as a variety of lively amusements.

Hardy's Wessex

These counties, together with adjoining areas, formed the ancient kingdom of Wessex of which Winchester was the capital city. It was the nursery of that great English spirit personified by Alfred the

Great, the most famous of the Cerdic rulers, the annals of whose kingdom have much enriched our history.

This region is also Thomas Hardy's 'Wessex' and devotees of the great writer will enjoy rediscovering the scenes he immortalised in his major novels and poems. Thomas Hardy had great powers of observation, and wrote wryly in a poem called *Afterwards* that he would like to be remembered as:

'A man who noticed such things'

What he noticed, of course, and expressed in language of matchless power, was the transient nature of all beauty and the irony of all human pretensions in the face of time. Yet there is a double irony in the fact that this melancholy poet and writer has ensured that 'Wessex' as he knew it has had immortality bestowed upon it by his pen.

Exploration of these counties is easy, and access from any part of Britain, extremely good already, continuously improves, with motorways pushing out tentacles ever nearer to the south coast, and with fast trains increasingly available.

PHYSICAL SETTING

Hampshire has a wide variety of attractive scenery, with splendid panoramic view-points among the downlands, pleasant river valleys, water-meadows and rustic villages. It is also well-wooded in many parts, while historic old towns afford additional interest.

Blackmore Vale

Blackmoor Vale in north Dorset is, perhaps, best known for its lush pasturelands and peaceful settings. Here there are fine water-meadows and much rich agricultural land so loved by Thomas Hardy who called it 'The Vale of the Little Dairies' in *Tess of the D'Urbervilles*.

'Egdon Heath'

Marshwood Vale in the west, is of a rather different character, narrow and enclosed, austere and lovely in a different way. The Rivers Frome and Stour with their tributaries, flow through delightful valleys and by thatched villages and ancient 'dreaming spires'. Between Dorchester and Poole lies the wild sprawl of heather, gorse and bracken which forms the Great Heath—the 'Egdon Heath' of Hardy's novels.

New Forest

In the south-west corner of Hampshire lies the New Forest, some 140 square miles of ancient forest-land which has long attracted those who enjoy outdoor activity. About half the New Forest is glorious woodland, while the remainder consists of wild, open heathland (where the gorse, heather and bracken flourish), and deep meadows dotted with thickets. A number of rivers and streams water the area and there are fine view-points from the uplands to the north.

Chalk Downs

The chalk downs of Hampshire range from near the Berkshire border, then, south of Basingstoke, to the north and west of Alton, and south again nearly as far as Petersfield. Chalk hills are found between Winchester and Salisbury, in Wiltshire, and again in the east where the extremity of the South Downs penetrates into the county around Butser Hill, 888 feet.

Pilsdon Pen

Running east to west like a huge backbone across mid-Dorset, the grassy downlands extend from west of Blandford Forum to the Devon boundary west of Broadwinsor, reaching over 900 feet at Pilsdon Pen (the western extremity), and a similar height at Bulbarrow Hill in the east. Many ancient camps and graveyards, or barrows, may be discerned by the trained eye along these grassy heights.

Another range of chalk hills extends east to west from Studland, near Swanage, to Abbotsbury in the west, embracing the Purbeck Hills and other stretches among which is Blackdown, affording many beautiful panoramic views towards the coast and Portland Harbour. In the extreme north-east of Dorset is Cranborne Chase where the downs rise to well over 800 feet.

Hampshire Rivers

The many rivers of Hampshire afford some of the finest angling in Britain. Along the banks of these pretty waterways lie fine water-meadows and here and there are thatched villages where the cottages cluster about a Norman church as they have done since the coming of those formidable henchman of William the Conqueror, in the eleventh century.

COASTAL RESORTS

With so many rivers and natural harbours it is inevitable that Hampshire's seaside resorts should be especially attractive to sailing enthusiasts. Southsea is the premier resort here, but Hayling Island, Lee-on-Solent, Lymington and Milford-on-Sea also attract many people who like 'messing about in boats'.

Bournemouth

Few counties can rival Dorset for its beauty and for the number and variety of its coastal resorts. Bournemouth, rightly regarded as the 'Queen' among them with its stately setting among the pines and rhododendrons, and with its cliffs pierced by the famous 'Chines', is a judicious combination of the old and the new. Poole too, is both

'ancient and modern' with its truly magnificent harbour, while
Christchurch is a fine yachting centre.

Lulworth Cove

Then there is Lulworth Cove and the lovely beaches near it which
may only be reached by boating or swimming. On the eastern side
of the Cove is the 'Fossil Forest' (accessible to those active enough
to tackle a short climb up the cliff), while along the coast proceeding
westward, there are small places like Ringstead with its wide,
delightfully sandy bay.

Weymouth

Weymouth's great bay sweeps in a wide arc, its fine sands
catering for old and young, and Portland (reached by the causeway
from Weymouth) has its famous Lighthouse on Portland Bill, the
great naval harbour, and the endless fascination of its little villages
with their steep streets. The people of Portland too, seem just that
little bit 'different'.

Chesil Beach

Between Weymouth and the charming Swannery at Abbotsbury
lies the marvellous natural breakwater of the Chesil Beach, 18 miles
of heaped pebbles washed in by the tides, and of varying shapes
and sizes, but averaging some $3\frac{1}{2}$ inches in diameterl Beyond the
Chesil Beach lie West Bay and Charmouth, tiny resorts nestling under
the shining sandstone cliff called Golden Cap. West of Charmouth
is Lyme Regis, historic, elegant and still with a faint aura of its
eighteenth-century watering-place popularity.

INDUSTRY

Dorset is largely a farming county with some admixture of
commerce since the Second World War in the shape of small pockets
of industrial development in places like Poole, famous for its pottery,
or Winfrith with its great Atomic Power Station. Across the border
in Hampshire there is the international port of Southampton and at
Fawley the massive oil refineries, Eastleigh with its railway works,
and the aircraft industry in Christchurch, along with many other
commercial enterprises which provide added employment
opportunities to people once dependent upon agriculture.

Holiday Trade

Catering for the holiday visitor is, perhaps, the most important
single industry in the coastal region. Bournemouth and Poole are
devoted almost entirely to this pursuit; Weymouth is a leading
resort, Lyme Regis and Bridport are important in the west, Swanage
is beautifully situated to the south of Poole, while Lymington, on
the Solent, is a fine yachting centre. In the east Portsmouth and

Southsea are renowned. Principal holiday centres somewhat further inland are Winchester and Salisbury because of their famous cathedrals. Sherborne and Shaftesbury also attract popular attention.

HISTORY

This part of England was the most thickly populated part of the country in prehistoric times as many memorials show. Among the most famous are Old Sarum in Wiltshire and Maiden Castle just outside Dorchester. Although so much of the country was wooded in those far off times, the present New Forest is a survival from a hunting chase planned and planted by William the Conqueror for the sport of himself and his followers.

The Romans

The first military adventurers to land in any force were the Romans who came in the first century and stayed for nearly four. Winchester (Venta Belgarum), Old Sarum, Dorchester (Durnovaria) and Ilchester (Lendiniae) were among their most important centres, together with the port of Southampton which they called Clausentum.

Saxon Times

After the Roman withdrawal in 410 the Britons were left to fend for themselves and soon found that they and their country were the natural targets of fierce tribes from the mainland of Europe, namely the Angles, Saxons and Jutes. A series of victories established the Anglo-Saxons in this area, Cynric defeating the Britons at Old Sarum in 552, and at Barbury Hill in 556. In later battles the Saxons penetrated westward into Somerset with some of their number settling permanently around Southampton Water and along the Dorset coast. It was in A.D. 676 that the episcopal seat at Dorchester-on-Thames was moved to Winchester, the capital of the by now largely Christian southern region. Sherborne became the head of another diocese in the year 705 but the seat of this bishop was transferred to Salisbury after the Norman Conquest.

Danish Invasion

Long before this more civilised state of affairs, however, the Angles, Saxons and Jutes had been battling with the invading Danes. The latter continued to push westward until at last Alfred the Great defeated them in Somerset and later at Edington in 878. After the treaty known as the Peace of Wedmore the advance of the Danes was halted, and within half a century more they were driven out of the region altogether.

After the Conquest

One of the benefits of the Norman Conquest was that before long the Conqueror's firm rule restored a certain peace and security to life in the southern counties, the effects of which lasted until about 1139 when the war between Stephen of Blois and his cousin Matilda over the throne of England brought back the nightmare of civil war, and a reminder of the Dark Ages. But with the rule of the Plantagenet kings stability returned to a certain extent and down the next centuries England grew into a considerable sea power.

Spanish Armada

In 1588 England's naval supremacy brought about the downfall of the huge Spanish Armada sent to invade her shores and such damage as had been inflicted during the running fights at sea was further increased by stormy weather. The attacks continued up the Channel to the eastern waters until the battered Spanish ships, that had set out so proudly from Spain, scattered round our coasts in an effort to escape into the Atlantic. Many were wrecked off the shores of Scotland and Ireland.

Stuart Times

In the seventeenth century a long period of peace ended with the Civil War between King and Parliament. Dorset and the west generally was largely Royalist in sympathy but the Roundhead forces triumphed finally, notably at Alton in 1643 and at Cheriton, near Winchester in 1644. Lyme Regis, held for the Roundheads, successfully defied a Royalist siege for a long period in 1644 but was not again involved in trouble until after the death of Charles II when the Duke of Monmouth made his abortive attempt to wrest the throne from James II. Received triumphantly at Lyme, Monmouth was routed at Sedgemoor in Somerset.

Rural Life

For the next two centuries life in places like Hampshire and Dorset was comparatively placid, and certainly in the remoter villages almost like an enclosed community. The livelier centres that had garrisons, like Weymouth or Dorchester, felt the effects of the Napoleonic Wars, through the comings and goings of regiments, while the country folk felt its effects through the Corn Laws and the blockade of the ports. After the defeat of Napoleon the villages and hamlets sank back into rural obscurity as reflected in the novels of Thomas Hardy, where the folk of one little community were scarcely acquainted with others who lived beyond the next valley and only the 'Tranter' or carrier, or the other travelling pack-salesmen brought news from far afield.

Roads and Railways

This remoteness was shattered ultimately by considerable improvement in roads so that coach services became more frequent and reliable, and the coming of the railway opened up the southern counties to people from much further afield.

WALKING

Dorset and the New Forest region have a wonderful variety of walks to offer. One can follow the coastline in many places, stroll by river banks, or meander over the many miles of chalk hills and downlands. In the New Forest especially, there are many and varied woodland walks. Near Southampton Water, or on the Solent, there is invariably a chance to see the great liners which sail to and from America. In north Dorset or South Wiltshire it is possible to explore the downs in glorious solitude, possibly not meeting other people for hours at a time.

CYCLING

Hampshire, even in the chalk down areas is an ideal county for the cyclist because the hill slopes are undulating rather than steep, while in the south there is much level terrain, especially in and around the New Forest. Dorset, perhaps, requires a little more study and careful preparation by the cyclist in order to avoid the many long climbs of more tediously steep inclines which can be encountered there. On the other hand there is little to rival the immense pleasure of travelling the quieter, secondary roads and lanes, although here too, there is ample reward for a little time expended in preliminary study. The dedicated cycle-tourist, armed with a good map and a well-prepared route may well see the southern counties to greater advantage than any other visitor. The views from the chalk downs, from the Purbeck Hills, and on the Portland peninsula are unforgettable for the rider, making the effort well worthwhile.

MOTORING

Dorset and Hampshire may be very pleasantly explored by car. The roads and lanes of the west side of the region are, in places, notably around the Lyme Regis area, likely to be more steep and twisting than those in the eastern part. Nevertheless the charm of the west far outweighs the small disadvantages of coping with these peculiarities.

From any one of the many attractive holiday centres it is easy to explore all parts of Dorset and Hampshire, although obviously, a fairly central stopping place has most advantages. The major roads are best avoided at week-ends in the summer season as there is often a considerable build-up of traffic with resulting time-consuming congestion.

Camping and Caravanning

A camping holiday can be great fun. It is often an excellent solution for families with lively, active children who find the atmosphere of hotels restrictive. It has the additional advantage of being inexpensive. If you wish to camp in a field it is obviously correct and courteous to obtain permission from the farmer or owner before attempting to pitch a tent or park a trailer-caravan.

The growing popularity of this form of holiday has ensured that there are today plenty of sites available and information on this score is now readily obtained from such sources as the Camping Club of Great Britain and Ireland, the two big motoring organisations (the A.A. and the R.A.C.), as well as several inexpensive publications covering the field.

ACCOMMODATION

A variety of accommodation of all types is available in the area; around the coastal resorts the supply is augmented by caravan and chalet camp sites where the lodging of your choice may be hired.

All resorts have a wide range of accommodation from the luxury hotels, often standing in their own grounds and commanding fine views of the surrounding countryside or coast, to well-appointed but modest guest-houses.

Many inland villages have small inns which cater for a limited number of guests while in more and more places furnished flats are available for renting. Private houses and country cottages often advertise 'Bed and Breakfast' accommodation and in some isolated areas, farmhouses will provide lodging for the visitor.

However, particularly in summer, between July and August, it is advisable to book accommodation in advance, or to decide one's overnight stop early in the day, before the 'NO VACANCY' boards appear.

THE NATIONAL TRUST

This now widely acclaimed organisation was founded in 1895, the brain-child of Miss Octavia Hill, Canon H. D. Rawnsley and Sir Robert Hunter. Their idea was to call a halt to the destruction of the unspoiled English countryside, towns and villages, by the ever remorseless march of industrialisation.

They decided to call their new movement 'The National Trust', and from the first it has remained unsponsored by Government, and has relied upon membership subscriptions, charitable donations and bequests.

A body of responsible people was formed to administer its funds, as trustees, acting for the people of the nation, buying lovely areas of countryside, so that they might be nature reserves as well as places of recreation, acquiring properties of archaeological interest, fine old houses, places with historic, literary and artistic associations, or any others which were threatened with destruction.

One of the glories of the work of The National Trust is the sensitive manner in which the properties have been maintained.

Some house unique collections of silver, china, or antique furniture: others have art galleries on the premises, and there are those like Clouds Hill, home of Lawrence of Arabia, set deep in the Dorset lanes north of Bovington Camp, which retain an intimate atmosphere, almost as though the former owner had just gone out and might return soon to his books and his famous collection of gramophone records.

The Parliament Act of 1907 conferred upon The National Trust the unique right to declare its lands, and most of its properties, inalienable — meaning that they can never be mortgaged or sold, nor compulsoirly acquired without the special permission of Parliament.

The general public has, as a rule, free access to the land owned by the Trust, and at properties where an admission fee is charged, there is a privilege free admission to Members of the Trust upon production of their membership cards.

Today the nation is vastly indebted to The National Trust for the preservation of whole stretches of glorious coastline which otherwise could have been despoiled, as well as all the other areas of great beauty or special interest.

ENGLISH TOURIST BOARD

A network of Tourist Information Centres exists throughout England. Each displays a sign, a red Tudor Rose with the words 'Tourist Information' on a blue ground. This is the symbol of the English Tourist Information Services.

Centres are categorised as follows:

NATIONAL (N)	like those at Bournemouth, Salisbury and Southampton which give information on every part of England.
REGIONAL (R)	offices which deal with the Tourist Board region in which they are located.
LOCAL (L)	where the staff answer only questions concerning purely local interest.
SPECIALISED (S)	centres where details on particular subjects, National Parks, The National Trust etc., are available.

Addresses and categories of these offices are quoted in this Guide.

Section 2   Bournemouth and East Dorset

BOURNEMOUTH

Population: 153,400
Early Closing Days: Wednesday and Saturday
Tourist Information Centres: (N) Tourism Department,
                                        Westover Road
                                        (L) Boscombe Information Centre,
                                        Royal Arcade, Christchurch Road

BOURNEMOUTH, QUEEN OF THE SOUTH COAST, faces due south and is noted for the pine trees to be found in all parts of the town.

Perhaps the best feature of Bournemouth is its sea-front: behind the esplanade rise cliffs with delightful chines, or ravines, running down to the sea. The town spreads over the cliffs and along the valleys, the centre being built along the valley of the Bourne Brook which is surrounded by parks and gardens for much of its length.

Bournemouth has little history: as recently as 1810 there was nothing but open heathland between Poole and Christchurch, common land now covered with pines which was similar to that surviving to the north and west at the present time.

Bournemouth was founded by Lewis Tregonwell, a Dorset squire who visited the site in 1810 and then built a summer residence there. The mild and equable climate attracted visitors, but even in 1841 there were only twenty-six buildings, and this number included a boarding house, a church, an hotel and a library.

Development

The railway, which usually brought about the rapid development
of seaside towns, passed Bournemouth by when the Southampton
and Dorchester line was opened in 1847, and when the railway
eventually arrived in 1870 it was merely a branch line from Ringwood,
via Christchurch. By this time there was a pier, and the town was
beginning to grow. In 1874 a line was built from Poole to
Bournemouth, but terminated at a different station. Only in 1888 was
the direct line opened. Two years later the population had grown to
37,000, and in 1918 the town became a parliamentary borough. Now
Bournemouth welcomes visitors from all over Western Europe.

Famous Names

Although it has such a brief history, several well-known people
were residents of Bournemouth. In St. Peter's Church, William
Godwin, an early political thinker is buried, together with his wife,
Mary Wollstonecraft an equally early protagonist in the fight for
women's equality. Their daughter Mary who married the poet Shelley
is also buried here, and the poet's heart lies in the grave of his son
Sir Percy Shelley. John Keble, a leader in the Oxford Movement,
lived in Bournemouth, as did Robert Louis Stevenson, from 1884 to
1887.

Along The Front

The sea-front at Bournemouth, with its miles of magnificent sands,
is most attractive. Below the cliffs runs an esplanade which gives
easy access to the romantic chines, whilst at the top is a drive which
extends almost along the whole length of the beach. From here there
are splendid views across to the Needles, the impressive chain of
rocks which form the western extremity of the Isle of Wight.

The Esplanade

The esplanade commences at Alum Promenade in the west,
where it is used only by pedestrians. Beyond is Branksome Dene
Chine, Alum Chine the most famous of them all, then Middle Chine
and Durley Chine. Bournemouth town centre itself is the
comparatively large chine down which runs the Bourne Brook.
Over a mile to the east lies Boscombe Chine. There are cliff railways
up the West and East cliffs in Bournemouth, and a third at
Boscombe-Southbourne. There are piers at both Bournemouth and
Boscombe.

At regular intervals along the esplanade, zig-zag paths connect
with the overcliff drive above.

The esplanade has various names. West of Bournemouth Pier it
becomes in turn Alum Promenade, Durley Promenade and West
Promenade. Between Bournemouth and Boscombe Piers it is called
Undercliff Drive and to the east of Boscombe Pier, Boscombe
Promenade, Southbourne Promenade and Solent Promenade. It

terminates a mile and a half west of Hengistbury Head, which marks
the eastern extremity of Poole Bay.

West of Bournemouth Pier and east of Boscombe Pier the
promenade is reserved for pedestrians, but between Bournemouth and
Boscombe Piers wheeled traffic is allowed between 1st October and
30th April.

Famous Pines

The centre of Bournemouth, and the residential suburbs, have
wide tree-lined streets with a very large proportion of pine trees:
there are several kinds, the most common being the Scots (*Pinus
sylvestris*), with a fine scent and golden bark, the Clustered Pine
(Pinus pinaster), which has large black cones, the Black Pine
(*Pinus nigra*) with very dark green leaves, the Corsican Pine (*Pinus
laricio*), with long narrow leaves, and the Remarkable Pine (*Pinus
insignis*). All these pines are to be seen throughout the town.

The Square

Much of the cultural and commercial life of Bournemouth is
concentrated near The Square. In Westover Road there are no fewer
than four places of entertainment: two cinemas, the Ice Skating
Rink, and the Palace Court Theatre. On the other side of the road is
the back of the Pavilion, with its theatre, dance-hall and restaurants.
West of the Pavilion in the Lower Gardens is the sheltered Pine Walk
leading to the Pier, at the end of which is the Pier Theatre.

The Russell-Cotes Museum and Art Gallery, and the Rothesay
Museum are near the Pier.

Winter Gardens

On the west of the Lower Gardens, on Exeter Road, are the famous
Winter Gardens, home of the famous Bournemouth Symphony
Orchestra, and the musical centre of the south of England.

Old Christchurch Road leads steeply up from The Square to the
Lansdowne where it meets Bath Road which comes up from the
sea-front. North of Old Christchurch Road is Horseshoe Common.

St. Peter's Church

Gervis Place runs roughly parallel with Old Christchurch Road,
and where it meets Hinton Road stands St. Peter's, the mother
church of Bournemouth. It is in an inconspicuous position, as it is
surrounded on three sides by shops and offices. It is surmounted by
a spire 202 feet high. The church was designed in its present form
in the years 1851 to 1879. Edmund Pearce and then G. E. Street were
the architects who enlarged the church, the first structure having been
erected on the site of two cottages which were originally used as a
place of worship.

At the base of the spire will be seen figures representing SS
Augustine, Ambrose, Gregory and Jerome, four Latin doctors of the

church. These were removed from their original position on the south porch of Bristol Cathedral after a short time, as Protestant feeling was so strong in that city.

The interior of the church is, perhaps, too richly decorated for some, but it is typical of a Victorian place of worship. The Liberal Prime Minister Gladstone made his last communion here. The south transept where he used to sit is now a chapel which bears his name.

R. L. Stevenson

The three chines penetrate much of the way from the coast to Poole Road. Alum Chine is the longest, being nearly three-quarters of a mile in length. It has fine yellow cliffs covered with heather and is crossed by a bridge connecting Beaulieu Road with West Overcliff Drive. On another bridge, between Alum Chine Road and Grosvenor Road, is a bronze plaque commemorating Robert Louis Stevenson who lived at Skerryvore, Alum Chine Road, from 1884 to 1887, during which time he wrote *Kidnapped*, *Dr. Jekyll and Mr. Hyde*, and *A Child's Garden of Verse*. The house was destroyed during the Second World War and the site has been made into a memorial garden. Near the top of the chine is the church of St. Ambrose.

Other chines are Middle Chine, crossed by a bridge carrying the West Overcliff Drive, Durley Chine, and two minute chines called Little Durley Chine, and Water Chine.

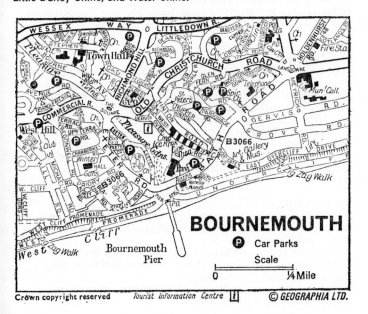

BOURNEMOUTH

Bournemouth Pier

P Car Parks

Scale
0   ¼ Mile

Pug's Hole

To the extreme west of Bournemouth, west of Meyrick Park, is a small park with the curious name of Pug's Hole. The name is derived from a smuggler called Pug who is said to have hidden his contraband in this wood until the time was ripe for its disposal.

A mile to the north of Pug's Hole, and to the west of the suburb of Winton, is Talbot Village; it has five farms, some twenty cottages with an acre of ground apiece, a church, a school and several almshouses.

BOSCOMBE

Boscombe seems like a separate resort although it is, in fact, an eastern suburb of Bournemouth. It has its own pier with an excellent pavilion, and its own large chine.

There is a model yacht pond at the bottom end of pretty Boscombe Chine, and in the centre of Boscombe there is plenty to interest the visitor. At the junction of Sea Road leading up from the Pier, and Christchurch road, is Boscombe Arcade, 336 feet long. Here will be found the Information Bureau.

The area north of the railway contains sports grounds, the East Cemetery and King's Park which has an athletics centre. The extensive Queen's Park lies to the north of King's Park and has a golf links and a miniature rifle range. From here there are good views over the Stour Valley and New Forest.

POKESDOWN

Situated to the east of Boscombe, Pokesdown straddles the Christchurch Road. Its church, dedicated to St. James and opened in 1858, is the second oldest in Bournemouth. The name is thought to derive from Pixie's Down, or Puck's Down. On some undeveloped land north of the railway two Bronze Age barrows were unearthed in 1909. A late Bronze Age urn-field cemetery was found in 1928, and pottery discovered indicated that Britain had been invaded from Europe between 1100 and 500 B.C. Some of the pottery is on display at the Russel-Cotes Museum.

SOUTHBOURNE

Southbourne consists of a promenade on top of the cliffs and another, for pedestrians only, at sea level, connected by a cliff railway and zig-zag paths.

The views extend over both Christchurch Bay and Poole Bay and a vista from Durleston Head, near Swanage, and far as Hurst Castle on the Solent can be enjoyed.

There are a succession of sandhills along the coast which make an excellent playground for children.

CHRISTCHURCH

Population: 31,100
Early Closing Day: Wednesday

CHRISTCHURCH IS DOMINATED BY its lovely Priory Church, much of which dates back to Norman times, although some portions are earlier.

Although now almost merged with its younger neighbour Bournemouth, the town, which dates back to Saxon times, has retained its independence and remains a complete contrast to the busier resort.

The Priory, the castle ruins and the large amount of frontage on two rivers—the Wiltshire Avon and the Stour, give Christchurch a quiet contemplative air which attracts many visitors: additionally this is a good centre for journeys into the New Forest.

A Legend

Originally called Twynham, the town already existed in Saxon times, and the change of name to Christchurch is the subject of a legend which has come down through the centuries. This says that the location of the Priory was planned to be St. Catherine's Hill, a fine view-point two miles from the town. However diligently the builders toiled, their day's work was always mysteriously undone during the night and the materials moved to the present site.

When the builders took the hint given by this startling procedure they noticed the presence of a stranger who had joined their company: he ate nothing, and asked for no payment. When one of the great beams was accidentally cut too short, it was found on the following day to be not only the correct length, but also in its planned position. Naturally, this mysterious carpenter was assumed to be none other than the Carpenter of Nazareth, and both the Priory and the town were thenceforth called Christchurch.

Early English

Historical records tell us that the present church was begun in the reign of William II by Ranulph Flambard, Bishop of Durham and Chancellor to the king. The earlier work is Norman with later work in Early English style. The reredos, rood screen, and Lady Chapel were added in the fourteenth century: the tower and parts of the choir followed in the fifteenth.

At the Dissolution of the Monasteries in 1539 the Priory buildings were destroyed, but the Priory itself became the town's parish church. This building has many fine features. Good examples of Norman arches can be seen on the exterior around a turret on the north transept and on the wall nearby. There are very high arches in the nave. Under the tower in the north wall there is a monument to the poet Shelley. A magnificent stone screen with panels illustrating biblical characters and scenes divides the choir from the nave.

Miraculous Beam

Near the choir are the Lady Chapel and the Miraculous Beam, and there is some fine carving in the choir stalls, misericords and reredos.

The Chantries

There are several impressive chantries: in the south transept will be found the Harys Chantry and Draper's Chantry. In the former there is the figure of a hare, and the letters YS on one of the panels, a play on the name Harys. In the north choir aisle is the fine Salisbury Chantry, built for Margaret of Salisbury, niece of Edward IV. She, however, was not allowed to rest there, because one of her sons, Cardinal Pole, published an attack on Henry VIII, who retaliated by executing every member of the family he could find, including Margaret, who was buried in the Tower of London.

Norman Bridge, Christchurch

The Castle

A few yards to the north of the priory are the ruins of the castle built by Richard de Redvers, Earl of Devon, shortly after 1100. Little remains except the east and west walls of the Keep and the Castle Hall, built around 1160 by the second Earl of Devon. The Castle Hall is one of the rare pieces of Norman domestic architecture surviving in this country. Adjoining the Castle entrance is an old thatched house, now a shop, where the Court Leet was once held.

The Quay

The Quay is near the Priory Church as is the disused Monk's Mill. Close by is a Norman two-arched bridge over the Avon leading to the Convent Walk which goes along the Avon to the Town Bridge from which fine views of Christchurch can be obtained.

From the Quay there are boat trips through the harbour and to Hengistbury Head which divides Poole Bay from Christchurch Bay. The Double Dykes earthworks protect the peninsula between Harbour and sea, the Head being the eastern extremity. The area was explored in 1911–1912 by the Society of Antiquaries, and finds included over 3,000 Gaulish and British coins.

Nature Trail

Beside the Avon Bridge is the entrance to a Nature Trail which meanders across the Stanpit Marsh, whilst a mile or so to the south-east is Mudeford with two lovely sandy beaches and a quay at the entrance to Christchurch Harbour from which a ferry runs to Mudeford Sandbank. This is a recreation area of chalets and holiday bungalows, but from the Sandbank one may walk to the top of Hengistbury Head, a magnificent view-point.

HIGHCLIFFE-ON-SEA

Population: 7,650
Early Closing Day: Wednesday

HIGHCLIFFE ON SEA IS THE MOST easterly of the new resorts on the Dorset coast, and lies four miles from Christchurch. Unlike the other resorts it is built among pine trees on the top of a low cliff. The main street is part of the main road from Christchurch to Lymington.

There is an attractive chine to the east of Highcliffe known as Chewton Bunny. The church is situated in the west of the town, and nearby is the burned-out ruin of the nineteenth-century Highcliffe castle.

The Cat and Fiddle Inn on the road to Lyndhurst is one of the famous New Forest inns.

POOLE

Population: 111,500
Early Closing Day: Wednesday
Tourist Information Centre: (R) Municipal Buildings, Civic Centre

POOLE, SPLENDIDLY SITUATED TO THE NORTH and east of its
Harbour is both seaport and holiday resort. Steeped in history, and
covering an extensive area which includes Branksome, Parkstone,
Branksome Park, Canford Cliffs and Sandbanks, Poole and
Bournemouth merge to form a huge built-up area.

History

Poole Harbour has been the haunt of man since prehistoric times.
The Romans built a town where Hamworthy stands today and called
it Moriconium. The modern town was first settled in Saxon days
and suffered at the hands of the Danes and Norsemen. Canute's
invading fleet entered Poole Harbour in 1015, but landed at Wareham.

The first charter, granted in 1248 by the Crusader William
Longespee, still exists in the town's archives.

Under Henry III Poole became a depot for provisioning ships of
the Navy and it sent four vessels to the siege of Calais. In the days
of the first Elizabeth, Poole benefited from the raids on the Spanish
fleets, and in 1588 sent its own ships to help fight the Armada.

Because Poole supported the Parliament in the Civil War its walls
were demolished by Charles II on his restoration, except for one
postern gate built around 1483.

Today Poole is an exciting mixture, both a holiday resort and a
port, which handles a surprising amount of local goods.

Old Town

Most of the interesting buildings are to be found in the old town
of Poole, situated where Holes Bay empties out into Poole Harbour
along a narrow channel. Poole Quay is a busy place, and here can
be seen the Harbour Office, Town Cellar and King Charles' Inn,
formerly the New Inn, renamed because on 15th September 1665
Charles II dined with the Duke of Monmouth in a house nearby.
The Custom House is noted for its double staircase and Town Beam.

Poole Pottery is well known and the factory producing it is
situated on the east of the Quay. An exhibition of pottery is open
mornings and afternoons from Monday to Friday, and mornings only
on Saturday. Conducted tours of the factory are arranged, a small
fee being charged.

High Street

The High Street is the main shopping centre of Poole, and here
also will be found some interesting buildings. The Guildhall, built
in 1761, has, like the Custom House, a double staircase. There are

many other fine Georgian and Queen Anne houses nearby.

Not far from the Guildhall is the church of St. James, built in 1820 on the site of an earlier edifice. There is a tablet here commemorating the rescue by Captain Peter Joliffe of a Weymouth fishing boat from a French privateer which he drove ashore. Two decades earlier, Joliffe had entertained George Fox, founder of the Society of Friends, and as a result of this visit a strong Quaker community grew up in Poole.

Scalpen's Court

In the museum at the corner of High Street and South Road there is an interesting collection of birds, archaeological exhibits and ethnological objects, including finds from the Roman station of Moriconium.

Another place worth visiting is the Old Town House, or Scalpen's Court, from the name of an eighteenth-century owner, which was built in the fourteenth and fifteenth centuries and used as the Guildhall until 1572. It is now a museum of the past and present life of Poole.

French King

Near the Custom House a tablet records the landing of the French King Charles X at Poole in 1830, after the revolution which deprived him of his throne. The exact spot is in Hamworthy, on the other side of the harbour.

The present Municipal Buildings are modern and are situated at Park Gates East. The offices were moved here from the Old Municipal Buildings, once the residence of Sir Peter Thompson whose coat of arms can still be seen on this mid-eighteenth-century building.

The Harbour

Poole Harbour is a paradise for yachtsmen. It has an irregular and highly indented coastline: much of it is sand and mud at low water and there are many islands, Brownsea being the largest.

Nature Trails

Brownsea Island, covered with miniature hills and valleys is a mile and a half long by three-quarters of a mile wide and has many groves of fir trees. It once belonged to the Abbots of Cerne and was also the site of the first experimental Boy Scout camp run by Lord Baden-Powell in 1907. The island now belongs to the National Trust and is reached by boat from Poole Quay or Sandbanks. The five hundred acres of woodland and heath, a reconstructed sixteenth/seventeenth-century castle, two lakes, a heronry, peacocks, ornamental pheasants and a Nature Trail afford scope for a wonderful day's outing. A small fee is charged.

The southern coast of Poole Harbour is very much indented and

very isolated. Here are the dead villages of Ower and Wych, and the
little village of Arne which is known for its nature trail.

The ceremony of Beating the Bounds of Poole, which includes the
harbour, was revived in 1921. During this operation a fleet of small
boats makes its way around the long coast of the harbour.

Parkstone

Hamworthy, to the west of Poole, is on the site of the Roman
settlement. Its chief feature is the huge power station with its two
tall chimneys. The church of St. Michael was rebuilt in 1959. The
much older rectory dating from 1610, where both Oliver Cromwell
and the Duke of Wellington lived for a time, is now part of the school
adjoining it. Rockley Sands holiday camp is nearby.

East of Poole Park with its two lakes and model railway is
Parkstone, a residential area, much of it consisting of pleasant
houses with large gardens, and streets lined with pine trees. The
chief feature of Parkstone is the fine modern church of St. Peter.
Broadstone is a residential area north of Poole, where the naturalist
Alfred Russel Wallace is buried in the churchyard.

Branksome Chine

An important feature of Branksome is The Avenue, with wide banks
of pine trees and rhododendrons running southwards to the coast.
Near to where it meets the sea is the lovely Branksome Chine, with
luxuriant vegetation including magnificent rhododendrons. The
smaller Branksome Dene Chine lies to the east of The Avenue.

Branksome has a promenade, but this is quite separate from that
of Bournemouth, as there is a gap of about half-a-mile where the
cliffs meet the sands.

Canford Cliffs

Canford Cliffs lies to the south of Parkstone and Branksome,
between Poole Harbour and Bournemouth. It is divided from
Parkstone by a golf course. This place has been developed in
recent years and is situated on breezy heathland on top of the cliffs.
The most interesting feature is Compton Acres with its ornamental
gardens, seven types in all, English, Italian, Japanese, Roman,
heather, Palm Court, and rock and water. Additionally there is a truly
magnificent view over Poole Harbour. Canford Cliff and Flag Head
chines run down to the sea, where a promenade fronts the beautiful
sands which provide fine bathing facilities.

Sandbanks

Sandbanks is at the end of the long spit of land dividing Poole
Harbour from the open sea. From here a floating bridge carries
vehicular traffic to Studland. Sandbanks has become a busy resort,
has fine sands, and offers excellent bathing, boating, and yachting
facilities, as well as trips to Brownsea Island.

WIMBORNE MINSTER

Population: 5,000
Early Closing Day: Wednesday
Market Days: Tuesday and Friday

WIMBORNE MINSTER IS A PLEASANT little town, situated on the
River Allen where it flows into the Stour: it is famous for its Minster
whose two towers are a prominent feature of the town.

One of the oldest settlements in the district, Wimborne was a
town in early Saxon days and rose to prominence when a nunnery
was founded by Cuthburga, Queen of Northumbria, who had fled
from her husband because of his cruel treatment to her. This was
in A.D. 705. The nunnery was destroyed by the Danes in 1013 and
Edward the Confessor built a college of secular canons on the site:
this was suppressed at the Dissolution of the Monasteries in 1539.

Wimborne was both an ecclesiastical and trading centre, linen
and cloth being made here from the days of the Saxons until after
the Restoration of Charles II when the place began to dwindle in
importance.

The Minster

Cruciform in shape the Minster was begun under the Normans and
remained after the college of secular canons disappeared. The lowest
of the four storeys of the central lantern tower formed a portion of
the first church. The quarter Jack is to be seen high up on the north
side of the western tower with a bell on each side on which he
strikes the quarters. Once a monk, the figure is now dressed as a
British Grenadier of Napoleon's day, but his tonsure can still be
seen under his soldier's head-dress. The western tower is the higher
but the design of the lantern tower is more ornate.

Astronomical Clock

The nave has arches in the Norman, Transitional and Decorated
styles: at the west end is the Baptistry, with a Norman font of
Purbeck marble, and on the south wall a remarkable orrery, or
astronomical clock built in 1325 by Peter Lightfoot, a monk from
Glastonbury: he made another for Wells Cathedral. The sun, moon
and stars revolve around the Earth, the sun giving the hour, and the
moon the lunar phases.

The choir has a fine east window with fifteenth-century glass in
the central panel. Here are the Beaufort Monument and a plate
recording the burial of Ethelred.

'Man in the Wall'

The Communion 'rail' consists of benches covered with linen cloths
which are a survival of those put out in medieval times for the elderly
and disabled. Another custom which survives is for the vergers to

walk around the Minster during the reading of the lessons in order to be able to tap with their wands of office anyone who has fallen asleep.

The south choir aisle, known also as the Chapel of the Holy Trinity, is used for weekday services. Here can be seen the 'Man in the Wall,' the marble coffin of Anthony Etricke, first Recorder of Poole, and famous as the man before whom the Duke of Monmouth was brought after the Battle of Sedgemoor in 1685.

The north choir aisle, or Chapel of St. George, contains the fine monument to Sir Edmund Uvedale, who died in 1606, and is commemorated by the 'dolefull duety' of his widow: there is also a Saxon chest. Another chest holds the deeds of charity lands invested in six trustees, each of whom holds the key to one of the six locks. A third chest contains parochial accounts going back to 1475.

The Library

The crypt, once the Lady Chapel, is reached by a flight of steps in the east of the south choir aisle. Part is reserved as a vault for the Bankes family, but a portion has been used for worship again, since 1922.

The Library, situated above the vestry, contains many treasures. These include a Breeches Bible (so called from the error in translation in Genesis iii, 7) a first edition of Sir Walter Raleigh's *History of the World* (somewhat damaged by fire, but repaired), a fourteenth-century manuscript on vellum, *Regimen Animarum*, Brian Walton's Polyglot Bible in seven languages, and churchwardens' accounts from 1403 to the present day, almost complete and among the oldest in the country.

There is also a fine collection of church music and a copper plate engraving of the Minster for the original edition of Hutchin's *Dorset*.

A visitor to the Library must be accompanied by a verger.

Model Town

Adjoining the Minster is the Church House, built in 1905, and the ancient Corn Market is situated nearby.

South of the Minster, in King Street, is an entrance to Queen Elizabeth's Grammar School, founded in 1496 by Margaret, Countess of Richmond and mother to Henry VII. Re-endowed by Elizabeth I in 1563, it was rebuilt in the nineteenth, and enlarged in the twentieth century. The school is mentioned in Hardy's *Two on a Tower*.

Another interesting feature is the Model Town. This depicts the central portion and includes the Minster, which can be illuminated from inside, and from which organ music can be heard. The model occupies 1,600 square yards and has 350 buildings. The floor of the Minster consists of 14,000 tiny tiles, and the gardens are planted with suitable alpine plants and miniature roses.

Leper Hospital

On the outskirts of Wimborne, on the Dorchester Road, is the Julian Bridge over the River Stour, and on the road to Blandford Forum is the Chapel of St. Margaret, once a Leper Hospital.

BADBURY RINGS

Situated three miles north-west of Wimborne Minster, this ancient earthwork and favourite beauty spot is reached from the B3082 at a point where a two-mile-long avenue of beech trees tends to screen the approach to the Rings, which lie on the right-hand side when proceeding towards Blandford Forum, and are reached by gravel and grass tracks. The extensive, bush-clad mounds and the deep ditch give access to delightful view-points and also overlook the point-to-point racecourse.

Tropical Birds

One mile to the south of Wimborne are the Merley Tropical Bird Gardens which are open daily during the summer season.

SWANAGE

Population: 8,500
Early Closing Day: Thursday
Tourist Information Centre: (R) The White House, Shore Road

SWANAGE IS A CHEERFUL, small but bright resort facing east over Swanage Bay and Poole Bay to the Isle of Wight which lies about twenty miles distant.

The sweep of Swanage Bay is bounded by Ballard Point to the north and Peveril Point to the south. Away to the north-east, beyond Ballard Point, the eastern parts of Bournemouth, Boscombe and Southbourne can be seen, and, on a very clear day, the tower of Christchurch Priory beyond Hengistbury Head.

The centre of the town is old, has narrow streets, but much is now wide and spacious. As a port, Swanage dates back to Saxon times and earlier: its two main occupations having been fishing, and the quarrying and shipping of Purbeck marble and other stone found in these hills.

The marauding Danes captured Wareham in 875 A.D. but in 877 were forced to retreat under pressure from King Alfred, and those who fled by water were defeated in a great sea battle off Swanage.

The town appears as Swanic and Swanwick in Domesday Book. Seven centuries later the Spanish Armada was sighted off the coast (July 1588) in its running fight up-channel with the 'little ships' of England.

Swanage remained a small fishing and quarrying town until the railway was opened from Wareham in 1880: then it began to grow rapidly and developed into the attractive seaside resort which it is today.

Town Centre

The centre of Swanage is the High Street which runs down through the old town to the shore and continues to the piers. Shore Road leads along the water front to New Swanage. The Mowlem Institute is in Shore Road: here is a lecture room and county library built by John Mowlem in 1863. There is a geological map of the Swanage area outside, also the monument to the 877 A.D. Battle of Swanage, erected by John Mowlem in 1882, the pillar of which is surmounted by four cannon-balls, ammunition quite unknown in 877! of course.

The Piers

The Piers is a Y-shaped projection into the sea. The left arm is used by the many vessels which call at Swanage and has shelters and seats along it. The right arm is much older, having been built in the mid-nineteenth century for shipping Purbeck stone.

Clock Tower

The Royal Hotel is a conspicuous feature on High Street near the Piers. Behind it is Peveril Point Road, leading to Peveril Point. About half-way between the Piers and the Point is the Clock Tower, a Gothic medieval tower brought from London Bridge in 1865, and for many years without a clock face.

On the Point itself are a coastguard station and Lifeboat House (open daily). Fine views can be obtained from Peveril Point, northwards to Ballard Point and southwards over Durlston Bay to Durlston Head. The downs are a breezy open space to the south of Peveril Point.

London Mementoes

Many of the interesting buildings in Swanage are to be found in that part of High Street which runs uphill, inland from Institute Road. Here is the Town Hall, once a private house, with a façade removed from Mercers' Hall in London and inscribed 'Cheapside 1670, Swanage 1882'.

A side road near the Town Hall leads to the Old Lock-up, erected, as the inscription says 'For the Prevention of Vice and Immorality by the Friends of Religion and Good Order, A.D. 1803'.

A little further up the High Street, and on the opposite side of the road, is Purbeck House, where a convent school stands on the site of a monastery. There are granite chippings from the Albert Memorial in the tower, and other mementoes of London in the garden.

St. Mary's Church

The Mill Pond and the Old Mill House are further up on the left. On the right, Church Road leads down to St. Mary's Church, built mostly in the thirteenth century, and once a fort; the tower is partly Saxon. The clock and bells were given in 1881 by George Burt in memory of his wife. The church was enlarged in 1859 and 1908. One of the past vicars was Dr. Andrew Bell, 1801 to 1810, who, with his colleague Thomas Manwell, was a pioneer of the Madras system of education.

Great Globe

Durlston Bay stretches from Peveril Point to Durlston Head near which stands Durlston Castle, now a restaurant. Below it is the Great Globe, ten feet across and weighing forty tons. It is placed so as to show the position of the Earth in space. The continents are marked, and the stone benches around it indicate the points of the compass.

Tilly Whim Caves

South-west of Durlston are the old quarry workings, the Tilly Whim Caves, which are reached by a steep tunnel. The name comes from Tilly, the owner of the quarry, and Whim from the local name for any contrivance used for raising stone from a quarry.

Anvil Point, just beyond the caves, is named after the anvil-shaped rock, still to be seen just above the waves at high water. Here the coast turns west. There is a lighthouse which can be visited, also pylons marking one end of a measured mile on which the speed of ships is tested: pylons marking the other end are westward along the coast. A mile beyond these other pylons is the Dancing Ledge, a level stretch of rocks which causes peculiar wave action at high tide. There is a swimming bath in the rock here. A further mile westward, East Man and West Man rise on either side of a small ravine. East Man is the burial place of those who perished in the wreck of the East Indiaman *Halsewell* in 1786, described by Charles Dickens in *The Long Voyage*. There are entrances to disused quarries all along this stretch of coast.

Benjamin Jesty

A mile north of St. Aldhelm's Head, Worth Matravers has a very old church, dedicated to St. Nicholas of Myra, and built in Saxon and Norman times. Benjamin Jesty (1731–1810), the farmer who pioneered vaccination, is buried in the churchyard. Langton Matravers lies to the west of Swanage and has a church dedicated to St. George, built in 1876, but with a small tower dating from the thirteenth century.

Purbeck Stone Quarries

Between the two vilages are the Purbeck Stone Quarries, which can be visited. The stone is worked by hand because blasting is not allowed. The quarrymen belong to one of the oldest of trades unions, the Ancient Order of Marblers in the Isle of Purbeck. Stone from these quarries has been used in many buildings, among them Westminster Abbey, and the cathedrals of Exeter, Salisbury and Winchester.

Purbeck Hills

North of Swanage is the long line of the Purbeck Hills, chalk downs running inland from the sea, descending to the gap guarded by Corfe Castle and thence rising again to a high point above Tyneham (watch for the flagpole), where a parking place makes an excellent picnic spot.

From here there are many excellent views in each direction: NOTE PARTICULARLY, much of the Purbeck Hills is in the areas of Army Firing Ranges, and when the red flags are flying one should keep away. In practice, the roads between Corfe Castle and Lulworth are freely open at weekends and holiday times: eastward from Corfe Castle there are no restrictions. The eastern extremity of the hills is called Ballard Point from where glorious views may be enjoyed.

STUDLAND

A mile north-east of Ballard Point are Old Harry, and Old Harry's Wife, two rocks just off the Foreland, otherwise known as Handfast Point, which forms the southern limit of Studland Bay.

Studland is an unspoiled village in a fine setting. Its church, dedicated to St. Nicholas of Myra, is an almost perfect Norman building. A mile inland, in the heath country, are the Agglestone (Holy Stone) and Puckstone, two hillocks composed of Ironstone.

Nature Trails

The road north from Studland runs to Shell Bay where there is a ferry to Sandbanks for Poole and Bournemouth, passing Studland Heath with its two Nature Trails and an irregularly-shaped lake known as the Little Sea.

CORFE CASTLE

Corfe Castle occupies a striking position in a gap in the Purbeck Hills and lies on the road from Swanage to Wareham. It is dominated by the ruins of its Norman Castle. The centre of the town is the Square where there is a cross, on a fourteenth-century base, celebrating Queen Victoria's Diamond Jubilee: there are also a museum and the Town Hall.

The Castle

Corfe Castle, which is open daily, has a stirring history. In a previous building King Edward the Martyr was murdered by his stepmother Elfrida, in 978 A.D. so that her own son could become king. The present castle was built by the Normans and was unsuccessfully besieged by King Stephen. King John, Edward I and other sovereigns lived here until the time of Henry VIII who strengthened it.

Elizabeth I sold the castle to Sir Christopher Hatton, on whose death in 1635, it was sold to the Bankes family. Lady Bankes held the castle for the Royalists in the Civil War and it was not taken by the Roundheads until 1646, when it was blown up. The Norman work was so sturdy that the gunpowder used caused only partial damage: the stone which was brought down was used in the building of many of the houses in the village. The remains of the castle consist of the Keep and several other towers on the top of the hill, also ruins of the surrounding wall and towers.

Kingston, south of Corfe Castle, is unusual in possessing two churches: the first is Norman, and the second, a magnificent structure, was built in 1880 by the third Lord Eldon at a cost of £60,000. The architect was G. E. Street.

Chapman's Pool

Southwards from Kingston, and reached by a toll road, is Chapman's Pool, situated amid open downland at a break in the magnificent cliffs. The walk from the car park to the rocky bay is rather rough, but the splendid scenery provides ample compensation.

Blue Pool

Church Knowle is a village a mile to the west of Corfe Castle; here there is a small cruciform thirteenth-century church. Above the village is Knowle Hill, 476 feet, and to the west Ridgeway Hill, 655 feet, from which extensive views can be obtained.

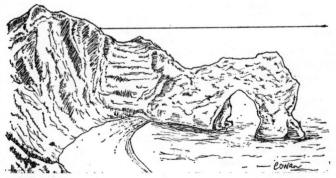

Durdle Door

Creech Grange is an old manor house in beautiful grounds to the north of the hills: peacocks from the grounds are often to be seen on the road which passes the Grange.

Kimmeridge, two miles from Church Knowle, is a village of thatched cottages, whose Church of St. Nicholas is a mixture of the Norman and Decorated styles. Kimmeridge gives its name to a clay which is found between the village and St. Aldhelm's Head, and in many other places. A mile north-west is Blue Pool, a beauty spot and picnic area at a lake of considerable size, surrounded by steep, fir tree-bearing slopes. Well defined paths encircle the lake and there is a small aviary.

WAREHAM

Population: 4,650
Early Closing Day: Wednesday
Market Days: Thursday and Saturday

WAREHAM IS A SLEEPY LITTLE TOWN of great antiquity standing at the western limit of navigation of Poole Harbour.

The Romans settled here, and built or strengthened the surrounding walls. During the Danish wars, Brictric, King of Wessex, was buried here in 800 A.D. and the town itself was sacked in 875, and again by Canute in 1015. In the civil war between Stephen and Matilda, the town was captured for the latter by Robert de Lincoln in 1138. Thereafter its history was more peaceful, and in 1703 Queen Anne granted it a charter. The town was rebuilt, without thatched houses, after a fire in 1762.

Wareham is surrounded by ramparts on all sides except the south where the River Frome flows. Just south of the bridge carrying the road from the railway station over the River Puddle is the ancient church of St. Martin. This is only forty-five feet in length and, traditionally, was founded in 705 by the first Bishop of Sherborne. The church was unoccupied from 1736 to 1936, apart from being used as a refuge in the fire of 1762, and for services commemorating the Jubilee of Queen Victoria in 1887. A statue of Lawrence of Arabia, in Arab dress, sculptured in 1939 can be seen in the church.

Lady St. Mary

The church dedicated to Lady St. Mary, in the south of the town, is in a mixture of styles and was rebuilt in 1882. In this church there are many features of interest, the most important being the Chapel of Edward the Martyr. Curiosities to be seen include stones which give the names of two of the Danish chiefs who sacked Wareham in 875 A.D. There is a walk around the old ramparts which are now laid out as a park:

Looking westwards from East Overcliff, Bournemouth

Lulworth Cove: sheltered beach with safe bathing

Reproduction of Hardy's study in Dorchester Museum

BERE REGIS

Bere Regis is a lovely village some six miles north-west of Wareham: the church here dates from Saxon times and includes work from many periods in its fabric. Perhaps its best known feature is the coloured and carved roof, given by Cardinal Morton who was born in the parish and died in the year 1500 when Archbishop of Canterbury. There is also a vault to the Turberville family who lived in a manor, part of which survives as Court Farm.

Lawrence of Arabia

Between Wareham and Bere Regis there is a large expanse of woodland known as Wareham Forest, and between the valleys of the Trent and Frome, south of the town, there is a wide tract of heathland called variously Bere Heath, Wool Heath, and Bovington Heath. To the west of this area, a mile north of Bovington Camp, is Clouds Hill Cottage, the last home of Colonel T. E. Lawrence (1888–1935). He was killed in a motor-cycle accident nearby; it is said that the sound of his motor-cycle (a Brough Superior) can still be heard in the quietness of early morning. The cottage was presented to the National Trust in 1937. It is a most remarkable dwelling-place. The bedroom (downstairs) is dominated by a great hide bed: the walls are covered with wonderful polished hides, leather hangings suspended like tapestries in a medieval manor house, but much more the decor of an Arab tent. This of course reflects the extraordinary personality of 'Lawrence of Arabia'.

Upstairs is the combined sitting-room and music-room, large and airy, lined with books and containing the Colonel's old gramophone and splendid collection of classical records. This too is, otherwise, furnished with spartan simplicity, and makes Clouds Hill very much the home of one who was that rare combination, the natural scholar and the man of action.

R.A.C. Tank Museum

South of the cottage is the extensive Bovington Army Camp. Here can be seen the Tank Museum where there are exhibits of tanks of all ages from many countries. T. E. Lawrence is buried in the churchyard at Moreton, one mile west of Bovington.

WOOL

The bridge over the River Frome is the chief feature in Wool: it is called Wellbridge by Hardy. The church here dates from the thirteenth century, although the tower is fifteenth. Bindon Abbey lies a quarter of a mile to the east, where the grounds are entered by a castellated gatehouse in red brick. Only the foundations of the Abbey remain: it was founded in 1172 by Robert de Newburgh, and housed monks of the Cistercian order. Here an empty stone coffin is to be seen: this is described by Hardy as the place where Angel Claire laid

c

Tess in the famous sleep-walking episode of *Tess of the D'Urbervilles*.

Two miles west of Wool is the Atomic Energy Authority power station on Winfrith Heath.

TOLPUDDLE

Tolpuddle, a few miles west of Bere Regis has its place in history as that where the Trades Union movement was born.

In 1834 George Loveless, Thomas Stanfield and several other farm workers were sentenced to transportation for forming a trade union which, at that time, was illegal. The village has many memorials to the 'Tolpuddle Martyrs': an arch in front of the Methodist Church was unveiled by Arthur Henderson in 1912, and six lovely thatched cottages were built and opened at the same time. In front is a dedication which reads:

'These cottages were erected by the T.U.C. as a memorial to the Tolpuddle Martyrs and may be inspected at the George Loveless Cottage'

PUDDLETOWN

This village is situated at the junction of the A35 with the A354, and is noted for its Perpendicular style church with 'Hardy associations'. It has a fine Jacobean Gallery, an old pulpit and font, and a panelled roof.

To the south-west lies Puddletown Forest which has a famous Rhododendron Mile' and a well-defined Nature Trail. When the rhododendrons are in bloom this is a 'mile' which should on no account be missed.

Westward lies Waterston Manor, a Jacobean manor house and the original of Weatherbury Farm in *Far From the Madding Crowd* in which Hardy immortalised the region all around Dorchester (his Casterbridge). The gardens at Waterston are open to the public on Sundays in summer.

East of Puddletown is Athelhampton Hall, a fine fifteenth-century and late Tudor mansion with a magnificent Great Hall furnished in period. It stands in ten acres of formal stone-walled and wild gardens. The house and grounds are open to the public on specified days during spring and summer.

LULWORTH COVE

This well-known beauty spot is a lovely bay encircled by cliffs, oval in shape with a small opening to the sea. There are pretty cottages at this much visited spot, plus curio shops and adequate parking.

West of Lulworth Cove are Nelson Fort and Stair Hole Cliff, containing the spectacular Cathedral Cavern and other caves. The beaches of St. Oswald Bay and Man o' War Bay with the Durdle Door, a natural rock arch, lie further west.

East of the Cove is a fossil forest, with the remains of Little Bindon Abbey on the cliff above. This ledge of limestone fossilisation of tree-trunks and tree-boles is accessible to those active enough to climb up from the east side of Lulworth Cove.

Beyond lies Mupe Bay, then Arish Mel Gap, and further on Worbarrow Bay. This latter is best reached from the Purbeck Hills when military restrictions permit.

Between the villages of West and East Lulworth stands Lulworth Castle, two miles from the Cove. Built in 1588 by the Weld family, who were Roman Catholics, it was burned down in 1929. East Lulworth parish church and a Roman Catholic church are situated in the grounds, and visitors are allowed in on Sundays, but should beware of fallen masonry in the castle ruins.

The bay at Ringstead is a quiet little spot where the National Trust controls three-quarters of a mile of the cliffs and coastline. There is a good car park, from which it is a short walk to the shoreline.

Memorial Stone

A path crosses the cliff-tops between White Nothe and Bats Head, in the area known as The Warren. Some way back from the cliff path, where there is a cluster of wind-bent thorn trees, stands the stone carved by Miss Elizabeth Muntz the sculptress, in memory of Llewelyn Powys, youngest of the famous literary Powys brothers. He lived for some years in a house called 'Chydyok' on Chaldon Down, just above the village of Chaldon Herring, and when his health permitted was usually about, walking over the downland or following the cliff-path. He died in a Swiss sanatorium just after the outbreak of World War II, but as soon as peace returned his ashes were brought home and buried where he had so loved to walk.

The stone bears his name, and the dates '1885–1939', while beneath are carved the words 'THE LIVING, THE LIVING SHALL PRAISE THEE.'

CHALDON HERRING

Lying along a country road between the A352 Wareham Road and Chaldon Down, just below the cliffs near White Nothe and Bats Head, Chaldon has been called the 'most secret village in Dorset'.

It was, for twenty years, the home of Theodore F. Powys, who was born in 1875, and lived until 1953. This second of the famous trio of literary brothers is considered by many to be the greatest genius of the family. His best known fiction includes *Mr. Weston's Good Wine*, *Mr. Tasker's Gods*, *Mockery Gap*, and *Unclay*. He also wrote philisophical studies such as *Soliloquies of A Hermit*. His style has the majestic power of biblical English, allied to ironic simplicity and mordant humour.

Section 3   Weymouth and West Dorset Coast

WEYMOUTH

Population: 41,500
Early Closing Day: Wednesday
Tourist Information Centre: (R) Publicity Office,
12, The Esplanade

WEYMOUTH, AN IMPORTANT SEASIDE RESORT, is most
beautifully situated in a wide, curving and sandy bay. It has grown
up round the mouth of the River Wey whose estuary widens out
west of the town to become the Radipole Lake. The town itself
nestles on the west curve of the bay, facing due east, and its
Esplanade sweeps round from the Pier (whence sail the boats to the
Channel Isles) up to Greenhill Terrace to the north-east.

Originally there were two villages, Weymouth to the south of the
Wey and Melcombe to the north, and in fact there were settlements
there in Roman times. Weymouth was the first to receive a charter
from the Norman monks of Winchester, long after the Conquest,

and Melcombe received one nearly thirty years later. Until the fourteenth century both towns returned separate Members to Parliament but their fortunes declined in subsequent years. A revival took place in Tudor times and in order to resolve the strong rivalry between the two neighbourhoods they were combined into the one borough of Weymouth in 1571.

Spanish Guns

A straggler from the defeated Spanish Armada was brought into Weymouth in 1588 and its guns were appropriated by the new borough to be added to the town's defences. In the years of the Civil War, the frail sense of civic pride in the town collapsed and at one point the two parts, Weymouth and Melcombe took opposite sides in the conflict. The place was dominated in turn by Royalists and Roundheads but declined considerably when the war was over, and continued to dwindle in importance and prosperity until the late eighteenth century when the idea of going to stay by the sea in the summer gradually took the imagination of those who could afford it.

Royal Visitor

It was George III who bestowed an accolade upon Weymouth by selecting it as the resort to which he went when convalescent from illness. Gloucester House, where the king stayed is still there, now an hotel. His presence with the queen and some of his daughters brought the town into new prominence so that it grew into a popular and fashionable resort. In the twentieth century the naval harbour at Portland played an important role in the two World Wars, suffering considerable bombardment during the Second. Nowadays this lively resort has been much expanded and is one of the most popular and important of the south coast holiday towns, welcoming visitors from abroad as well as from elsewhere in Britain.

Along the Front

From Greenhill Gardens in the east, the Esplanade goes via Brunswick Terrace (where, at Penn House, the famous literary brothers, John, Theodore and Llewelyn Powys spent many happy holidays in the home of their grandmother), on past the Alexandra Gardens, to the Pavilion Theatre and the busy landing stages by the Pier, for the boats to and from the Channel Islands.

Royal Terrace

Two landmarks distinguish the Georgian elegance of the Esplanade. One is the statue of its benefactor, George III, situated just opposite Royal Terrace; the other is the ornate Jubilee Clock standing opposite where King Street breaches Gloucester Road and Royal Crescent. The statue and the clock are each popular trysting places for young and old alike.

Shopping Centres

St. Mary's Street with its splendid Guildhall and St. Thomas's Street, fork slightly left, going south from the royal statue. St. Thomas's Street, usually thronged with visitors in the season, has the handsome Masonic Hall, built in 1815. It is Grecian Doric in style and owes much to the splendid craftsmanship of the Georgian plasterer who executed the work. At the end of this street is the Town Bridge over the River Wey, giving access to the North Quay where the mainly Victorian Trinity Church was the first one to be built on the 'Weymouth' side of the harbour. The area north of the Town Bridge was old 'Melcombe Regis'.

View From the Steps

Chapelhay Steps, beside Trinity Church, are worth climbing because from the top it is easy to envisage what the former twin towns must have looked like. A Chapel dedicated to St. Nicholas once stood on the space at the top of these steps. It was originally built in the fourteenth century as a Chapel of Ease for the old church in Wyke Regis, to the west on the Wyke Road, but during the Civil War it was converted into a fort. Too greatly damaged to be used again as a chapel, it was demolished.

Oldest Buildings

From Trinity Terrace behind the church, one can look down over the little houses facing the harbour. Some of the outbuildings in the gardens below the cliff are probably centuries old, in fact older than the quay wall! Steps down from the Terrace lead into Hope Square where Pilgrim House is noteworthy. It was reconstructed in the eighteenth century. In neighbouring Hope Street the building at number 6 is distinguished by its original Fire Insurance sign, still intact.

Trinity Street

On the western side of the former inlet the houses at numbers 2 and 3 have been carefully restored and are open to the public. They are of some quality and would have been superior to most of the tumbling hovels which characterised the harbour quarter in those days. Across the road is the 'Old Rooms Inn' a substantial Jacobean building which was once the centre of social life in Georgian days, for it became the Assembly Rooms.

Historic Stone

Trinity Road is mainly eighteenth century in its aspect. Behind the Cove Restaurant where a retaining wall helps to support the Trinity Terrace it is possible to see an old stone, triangular in shape and bearing the carved figure of a robed monk carrying staff and book. This is thought to have come from the former Chapel of St. Nicholas at the top of Chapelhay Steps.

Sir James Thornhill

Retracing one's steps over the Town Bridge, past the old warehouses in St. Edmund's Street, there stands in the next turning St. Nicholas' Street, a fragment of the old Victorian Theatre, its Entrance Archway. The building began life as a Congregational Chapel, became a theatre but was subsequently superseded by the Victoria Hall in 1887 (which later became a cinema).

Also in St. Nicholas' Street is the old White Hart Hotel which has connections with Sir James Thornhill the noted Georgian painter whose *'Last Supper'* is to be found at St. Mary's Church in nearby St. Mary's Street. Sir James was also for a time the Member of Parliament for Weymouth.

Stone Pier

On the south side of the Harbour and opposite the Pleasure Pier, lie the Nothe Gardens, which are a lovely sight in themselves, and an excellent view-point from which to look towards St. Alban's Head in the north and over Portland Harbour to the south. The Nothe Fort lies at the extreme end of this little peninsula and here, parallel with the Pleasure Pier across the water, is the Stone Pier.

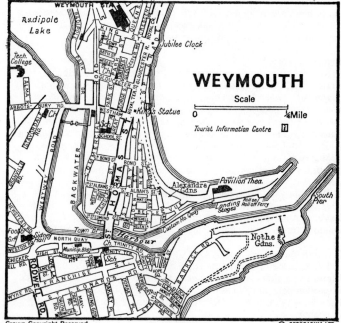

Crown Copyright Reserved

© GEOGRAPHIA LTD.

Sandsfoot Castle

The Portland Breakwater juts out from the end of Newton Road, on the western side of Newton Cove. This part of the coast has been made into a park, and it is here that there stands the ruined Sandsfoot Castle, a blockhouse built in 1539 by order of Henry VIII. Wyke Regis lies behind the coast here, and the mother church of Weymouth, high up on the Portland Road, dates from 1455, having replaced an earlier structure. In the churchyard is the grave of Captain John Wordsworth, the sailor brother of William Wordsworth the poet, whose ship was wrecked off the coast here.

Entertainment

Weymouth is a very lively holiday centre. Apart from its naturally attractive setting in the Dorset countryside, and the glory of its golden sands and wide bay, it presents a charming sight in its everyday aspect. The Corporation gardeners make splendid floral displays in the public gardens and along the promenade. In the Greenhill Gardens a speciality is made of symbolising great events of local importance. A superb one was the display which pictured in flowers the cottage at Higher Bockhampton where Thomas Hardy was born in 1840.

At night the chains of lights along the Esplanade and around the public gardens give a fairy-tale glow to the resort and there is a lively choice of dining and dancing establishments, shows at the Pavilion Theatre, and various restaurants, cafés and bars.

Grand Carnival

Not only the adults are catered for in the matter of outdoor amusement, though there are many interesting boating, water-ski-ing events and swimming galas on the seasonal calendar. For children there is the Punch-and-Judy Show which has always been a feature of entertainment on the sands in Weymouth; there are rides in the donkey-carriages and the new Model Village at Lodmoor which is still being expanded. Chipperfield's, in Westham, is the largest Amusement Park in Dorset and here there are all the children's favourites such as mat slides, roundabouts, swing-boats, the big wheel and a scenic railway.

Of interest to young and old alike are the Royal Navy's 'At Home' days when the public is welcomed aboard a ship of Her Majesty's Navy. In August a special additional attraction is the Grand Carnival which is noted for the variety and ingenuity of the colourful floats.

English Scene

In the harbour, behind the Quay and the Pier with the Channel Island ships, there are always many trim and attractive craft moored. Photographers, amateur and otherwise, are invariably to be found here, busy with their cameras, eager to capture this most English of scenes.

PORTLAND

Population: 13,750
Early Closing Day: Wednesday

THIS NARROW PENINSULA LINKED TO WEYMOUTH by a
causeway was called by Thomas Hardy 'the Gibraltar of Wessex',
and in his fiction it was disguised by the name 'Isle of Slingers'.
This was a reference to its famous stone so long quarried for famous
buildings elsewhere in the country. Sir Christopher Wren, who was
for a time Member of Parliament for Weymouth, knew the value of
Portland stone and used it for his great masterpiece, St. Paul's in
London, and many of his other churches in the city.

Portland Castle

The old breakwater, built in 1849–1872, extends northwards
from the eastern side of Portland to complete the enclosure of the
Harbour extending southward from Weymouth. About a mile
westward is Portland Castle, another of Henry VIII's Blockhouses
along the the southern coast. This one, unlike Sandsfoot Castle is
in excellent preservation, is lived in, and remains open to the public.

The Villages

Just south of the Castle is Castletown, and also Fortuneswell with
the Church of St. John, built in 1840. Verne, higher up along the
stony main road, was once a prehistoric settlement, and then a
Roman one. Neighbouring East Weare Battery is part of the defences
of Portland Harbour, for Portland is an important naval base.

Rufus Castle

Just south-east of the village of Easton is Church Ope Cove with
the ruins of a castle which once belonged to William II (Rufus).
Above the Cove is Avice's Cottage described by Thomas Hardy in
the Novel *The Well-Beloved*. Today it houses the Hardy and Portland
Museum which is, of course, open to the public.

Southwell is the most southerly village of the peninsula and St.
Andrew's church there was built in 1879 by people who knew the
passengers from the two ships *Avalanche* and *Forest* which sank
after a collision some twelve miles out to sea.

Portland Bill

The southernmost tip of Portland Isle, or peninsula, slopes gradually
down towards Portland Bill where stands the old lighthouse, now
used as a bird-watching station and open to the public. Here the
tidal races are very dangerous and currents of up to seven knots
can occur, making boating and bathing very dangerous. It is even
dangerous to stand too near the edge of the rocks at such times for
huge waves can rear up suddenly. The obelisk erected by Trinity

House marks the most southerly point of all. The Pulpit Rock, standing amid the swirling currents is one of the many unusual rock formations which distinguish the Dorset coast.

From the wide ledges of rock around the area where the lighthouse is situated it is possible on fine, clear days to enjoy splendid views out to sea, and often as far as the Shambles Lightship, marking the Shambles Sands, some five miles due east of Portland Bill.

Wishing Well

Originally a separate village, Upwey is now part of Weymouth. It is to the north of the resort, on the main Dorchester road. Just to the west of the main road, in a little valley, is the famous Upwey Wishing Well, where the waters were often used by George III. The pretty little nook where the well is situated is a favourite place with visitors who enjoy also the fun of duly making a wish.

Here too is the Church of St. Lawrence, largely Perpendicular in style and built in 1267. There is a Saxon font, and some fine Flemish glass dating from the fourteenth century. Out on the main road is the ruined Bayard Dairy, a Tudor house, and also the Manor House. The downs all around Upwey and neighbouring Corton are ideal places for walking or riding. Corton Farm, about a mile and a half west across the downs was once a medieval village with its own chapel. This last has been reconsecrated and occasionally services are held there.

Roman Villa

Broadwey to the South of Upwey, has a small church in Decorated style, and Nottington, a mile to the west was once a spa in its own right. Well House, which once contained the spring is now privately owned, Radipole and its fine 'swan lake' lie to the south of Nottington and the curious turret of Radipole Church is a landmark to be noted. This was once the mother church of Melcombe.

About two miles east of Upwey on the main road between Weymouth and Bournemouth, is the village of Preston with its fifteenth-century church. Near the church there is some interesting Roman paving which has been preserved in the spot where it was uncovered. The name of the village is said to derive from 'Priest Town'. Half a mile southwards, on the coast is Bowleaze Cove; nearby are the remains of a Roman Villa.

White Horse

Just north of Preston is the pretty village of Sutton Poyntz, the 'Overcombe' of Hardy's *Trumpet Major*, and on the hills between Sutton Poyntz and Poxwell is the famous image of a White Horse carved in the chalk in 1808 in honour of George III. West of Sutton Poyntz is Chalbury Hill, an Iron Age hill fort of considerable interest.

Poxwell Stone Circle

Poxwell on the A353 has, in a field just past the turning to Upton, an ancient Stone Circle which is like 'a miniature Stonehenge', as Llewelyn Powys wrote in an essay on the subject. The very tallest of the stones would be scarcely knee-high on a man, yet this ancient religious circle is the oldest place of worship in Dorset. To the sensitive imagination these lowly stones have a strange fascination, though their power is best felt at midnight, when the air is still and the leaves on the trees in Trenchard Wood are not stirred by the breeze.

Link With The Crimea

The valley below Chalbury is called Balaclava Valley in commemoration of the famous battle in the Crimean War of 1854–55. The Early English church at Bincombe, just west of Chalbury has an interesting Norman font, while at Whitcombe just beside the A352 north of Broadmayne, the church, dating from the thirteenth century is set among some notable earthworks in which the area abounds.

The 'Dorsetshire Burns'

Winterborne Came, which is set in charming country just south-east of Dorchester, had as its Vicar in 1847, William Barnes, the 'Dorsetshire Burns', so called because though he was a great classical scholar, Barnes became famous as a poet writing in the Dorset dialect. Indeed, he raised this dialect by his charming verses, just as Burns made 'lowland Scots' a vehicle for some of his most delightful songs. William Barnes' song *Linden Lea* is a favourite with singers and is known all over the world.

He lived in the thatched rectory and his grave, marked by a Celtic Cross, is in the churchyard close by, in the shelter of the church where he was the Minister for twenty-five years. It is a pleasant resting place for one who so loved the buttercup meadows, the 'shrouded elms' and sturdy oaks round about his home.

ABBOTSBURY

Nine miles north-west of Weymouth, at the end of the Chesil Beach, lies Abbotsbury, famous for its Swannery and Sub-tropical Gardens. St. Nicholas's Church is the principal building and is sixteenth-century Perpendicular in style. Among its interesting features are the seventeenth-century chancel ceiling, a representation over the west door of the Holy Trinity, an old man with a Crucifix and a dove, and the Pulpit with bullet holes dating from the Civil War. Opposite the church stands the handsome Manor House.

Ruined Abbey

The ruins of a Benedictine Abbey, dedicated to St. Peter, are still to be seen at Abbotsbury where they form part of the outbuildings of

Abbey Farm. The original place was destroyed in 1644 during the Civil War and archaeologists have long been interested in examining it. The pond with an island in it used to be the monks' fishpond and the enormous Tithe Barn was their granary. This Barn, heavily buttressed, dates from the thirteenth century and is 31 feet high and 276 feet long, probably the very largest such building surviving in England. St. Catherine's Chapel up on the hill above Abbotsbury is a fine fifteenth-century building built by the Benedictine monks. The view from the hill-top is splendid.

The Swannery

The Swannery at Abbotsbury is one of the oldest nature reserves in Britain for it has existed for 600 years. Cygnets are hatched out every year and swim in the waters of The Fleet which is brackish, so they come out to the Swannery to drink. The Swannery is visited also by many species of wild bird.

The sub-tropical gardens lie between the Bridport road and the sea. The entrance is easily found, about five hundred yards from the place where the road forks left, and in these extensive grounds there are some 7,000 varieties of sub-tropical plants which are on sale to the public.

Hardy Memorial

Admiral Sir Thomas Masterman Hardy, who was once Nelson's flag-captain, lived in Portesham which is still a charming, unspoiled village a little to the east of Abbotsbury. He was born at Kingston Russell, north-west of Dorchester, but spent more years in Portesham. High on Blackdown Hill, above the village, is Hardy's Monument marking the spot which was to become the old Admiral's favourite 'look-out post' across the waters of the Channel. The old hero who had been in the cabin of *Victory* as England's greatest Admiral lay dying after Trafalgar, regularly climbed up from the village to scan the waters which the 'Senior Service' had patrolled so successfully that in his day Britain seemed impregnable. Now the stone column of his memorial, erected in 1844, is a familiar landmark all over southern Dorset.

CHESIL BEACH

Chesil Beach extends for about 16 miles along the coast from Portland to Burton Bradstock. At its northern end it divides the small Burton Mere from the sea, but between Abbotsbury and Portland Harbour, it encloses the rather sluggish waters of the lagoon known as The Fleet. This is eight miles long and divided into West Fleet and East Fleet: at the western end the protecting Chesil Beach is 23 feet high and 170 yards wide while at Portland it is 42 feet high and 200 yards wide. The pebbles at the western end are small but increase in size towards the Portland end of this almost unique ridge.

There is a very dangerous undertow in the waters around it and the sea is very deep: so it is extremely dangerous to attempt bathing there.

DORCHESTER

Population: 13,800
Early Closing Day: Thursday
Market Day: Wednesday

DORCHESTER, THE DURNOVARIA OF THE ROMANS, was already a well-known settlement in the time of Stone Age Man, and in the Bronze and Iron Ages. Maumbury Rings at its western edge was a Stone Age circle, and this the Romans adapted to serve as their 'local' theatre. When the Romans left their northern provinces to get on as best they could, the Saxons became masters of Dorchester and by the year A.D. 925 and throughout the reign of King Athelstan it was the Saxon mint town. With the coming of the Normans life changed again in the town, for it became one of the favourite Plantagenet hunting seats and gradually established itself as a market town.

The Puritans

In the seventeenth century, John White, one of the notable Puritan leaders, led a party of immigrants to the New World in the ship *Mary and John* and this little group crossed the Atlantic successfully to found, in Massachusetts, a second Dorchester with their own church, free rom the persecution which had driven them from England.

Bloody Assize

The notorious 'Hanging Judge' Jeffreys here conducted a 'Bloody Assize' in 1685, when simple countrymen who had done no more than help a wounded man, or given a drink of water to a fainting soldier, were sentenced as savagely as those who had been part and parcel of the rebellion led by the Protestant Duke of Monmouth. Jeffreys' 'Lodging' is one of the historic buildings in the main road.

In the seventeenth century Dorchester was four times ravaged by fire so that the oldest parts of the place were largely destroyed. Its general aspect today is eighteenth-century and even in the present age of speed and hustle, it has an easy-going atmosphere of graciousness and charm like all the best country market towns.

Compact Town

Dorchester is a compact town with its High Street divided into East' and 'West', and contiguous with the London Road coming in from the east, and the Bridport Road leading out to the west. The centre of town is enclosed within Kings Road, Prince of Wales Road and Trinity Street and two main avenues leading southward are the Wareham Road and the Weymouth Avenue.

Tolpuddle Martyrs

The old Crown Court in High West Street was the scene in 1834 of the trial of the six men, all agricultural labourers, whose offence was, that having failed to resist a cruel reduction in their wages, they sought to form a Trade Union.

Brought before an unimaginative and perhaps rather ruthless Bench of Magistrates, condemned by the dubious testimony of spies and informers, these workers, so peaceable and so harmless, were sentenced to transportation to Australia for seven years. What that meant in terms of the suffering of their families and the heartbreak to themselves in those days of slow sea travel and indifferent postal deliveries abroad, can be imagined!

What comes down to us today from this pitiful story is the amazing dignity of the Loveless Brothers and their four workmates, and especially the bearing of George Loveless who was a religious man and a lay-preacher. He faced Mr. Baron Williams the presiding judge and uttered these memorable words at the end of the trial:

'My Lord, if we have violated any law it was not done intentionally. We were united together to preserve ourselves, our wives and our children from utter degradation and starvation.'

Happily, in Britain, even in those tough times, the strong sense of fair play soon asserted itself and there were endless demonstrations and representations about the monstrous injustice which had been seen to be done, so that the sentences were shortened, although even then, George Loveless only discovered by chance from an out-of-date newspaper that he and his companions were being held illegally in Australia! Still, they did come home again eventually and faithful Betsy Loveless rejoiced at last in having her husband restored to her.

Looking around the compact little Court House, and visualising the scene so long ago, it is strange to reflect upon the large drama enacted in such a homely setting. It is odder still to realise that few, if any, of the participants dreamed that their names would go sounding down the centuries in a story which would be told all over the world.

St. Peter's Church

The church which stands upon the corner of Carfax and at the junction of High Street West with High Street East is dedicated to St. Peter. Its square tower, 90 feet high, dominates Dorchester and the church itself stands upon the site of an earlier one. The present fabric is largely fifteenth-century and it incorporates the original south porch of the first church, it having been reconstructed, stone by stone, when the existing church was built.

Within the church are memorials to the Reverend John White, the founder of Massachusetts in New England, to William Barnes, the poet and clergyman, who was also an antiquary and philologist, Denzil Holles, of 'Long Parliament' fame (just before the Civil War), and, in the south aisle, the memorial to Thomas Hardy. This is the Hardy Memorial Chapel which also honours the great writer's ancestors. The pulpit and the reredos are other interesting features of the interior of St. Peter's. Outside the church is the statue of William Barnes who was born in 1801 (four years before the Battle of Trafalgar), and who lived until 1886, (when Victoria had been Queen for 49 years!). It was a truly remarkable life-span, covering so much historic change.

The Museum

The Dorset County Museum next door to the church in High West Street, has some extremely interesting exhibits connected with the history, the nature conservation and the archaeological finds in the county. Its prize exhibition, however, is the reconstruction of Thomas Hardy's study, as it was, in Max Gate, at the time of his death in 1928.

It is indeed, a most intimate experience to look through and see the old desk, with its blotting paper and writing materials, the author's pince-nez and other personal things. One of the most moving items is the small framed painting of an old shepherd, weather-beaten and brown, his old eyes full of the lore of the countryside. It was so much loved by the famous author that it hung always beside his bed and may even have been the last object at which he looked on that cold January day of his death.

Other Interesting Buildings

In High East Street is a very handsome Georgian inn, the King's Arms, which has fine bowed windows above the canopied porch, supported by four pillars. The Post Office in South Street has a fine ornamental plaque which was designed by Thomas Hardy in his young days, and opposite stand the Nappers Mite Almshouses dating from 1616. Next door to them is the Old Grammar School built by another Thomas Hardy in 1569 and remaining in use as a school until 1929 when the establishment moved out to larger buildings in the south-east part of town.

Literary Associations

Not only is Dorchester famous as Hardy's 'Casterbridge', celebrated in his book *The Mayor of Casterbridge*, it is of interest to book-lovers as having associations with the famous Powys family of writers. In South Walks on the southern edge of Dorchester there stood for

many years Rothesay House which was rented by the Reverend
Charles Powys when he took the post of curate to the vicar of St.
Peter's. Though he was already a vicar in Derbyshire, he took this
minor post in order to be near his aged mother, a widow bereaved
afresh by the loss of a soldier son in India.

Here John Cowper Powys remembered as a young boy peeping
from the grounds to see the Reverend William Barnes pacing under
the trees in his eighteenth-century dress, and silver-buckled shoes. At
Rothesay House, a pleasant early Victorian building standing in
atrractive grounds, Llewelyn Powys, youngest of the famous brothers
was born, and it was from this house that his mother took him over to
Winterborne Came to be blessed by old William Barnes. Though he
was only a babe in arms, the writer liked to think, in later years, of
how his mother had made this 'gracious pilgrimage with him, to
one who was so apt an interpreter of the Dorset countryside'. The
house has disappeared but those interested will find that the new
Telephone Exchange in South Walks marks where it stood.

Military Museum

West of Poundbury Road and out on the Bridport Road is the
Dorset Military Museum, housed in the Keep of the old Dorset
Regimental Depot. One of its most remarkable relics is the desk used
by Adolf Hitler from 1933 to 1945. It is strange to see this
business-like but homely piece of furniture from the Berlin
Chancellory which is nevertheless rendered extraordinary by its
association with one of the most monstrous figures in modern
history. The relics of an altogether different, and very English military
leader of genius, Clive of India, are of great interest.

The main display records the history of the Dorset Regiment
(Dorset Militia, Volunteers and Queen's Own Dorset Yeomanry),
from 1660 onwards, by means of illustrations, uniforms, medals,
weapons and battlefield relics.

Max Gate

Out on the Wareham Road, about three-quarters of a mile from
the town centre, is Max Gate, the home of Thomas Hardy in the
years of his success, and where he died in 1928. It is an
unpretentious Victorian villa standing in its own grounds. Of much
greater interest is the author's birthplace at Higher Bockhampton, a
little hamlet north-east of Dorchester. A pleasant route to this
delightful place is out via the London Road, over Grey's Bridge,
(where Hardy's Mayor of Casterbridge saw his own effigy floating
down the River Frome), through quiet lanes to the delightful thatched
cottage which is now the property of the National Trust.

The Birthplace

The cottage belonging to Hardy's father, a builder by trade, stood
in one acre of garden in the shadow of the neighbouring woods.

Harbour and The Cobb: Lyme Regis

St. Alban's Head: spectacular cliff near Chapman's Pool

Salisbury Cathedral seen from the south-west

The Cerne Giant: ancient fertility-cult figure

Just under one acre has been added to the land adjoining the cottage through the Groves Fund which made the purchase possible in 1967.

Some of the interior items belonging to the author's time were donated under the will of a Miss E. L. Evans, the property itself having been acquired originally in 1948. It is extremely fascinating to stand in this little house and recollect that according to the author's own account his first conscious memory was his spellbound contemplation of the shining body of a new kitchen kettle his mother had bought in Dorchester market.

The young Hardy used to sit in the window of an upstairs room (the one furthest from the tiny wicket-gate into the garden), absorbed in the books which fed his eager mind. To the eastward rolls, 'Egdon Heath', that ancient Wessex moorland which adds its own dimension to Hardy's writing and is the palpable embodiment of his view of life, with its soft beauty on the one hand and rugged almost savage wildness on the other.

Stinsford Churchyard

About three miles south-west from the cottage at Higher Bockhampton is Stinsford Churchyard where the heart of Thomas Hardy lies buried. He wished to be buried there but because of his supreme eminence in the world of literature it was decided that a compromise would be better. His ashes were taken to Poet's Corner in Westminster Abbey and his heart has its own tomb at Stinsford which he loved so much. There is a handsome Memorial Window to Hardy in Stinsford Church.

Maiden Castle

On the other side of Dorchester, just to the south-west, is Maiden Castle, an Iron Age hill-fort, protected at its south-east extremity by a double bank with a shallow ditch between. One of the most amazing Iron Age relics in the country, Maiden Castle covers some 120 acres of ground and it is reckoned that something like 5,000 people in number could have been protected within its fortifications. Evidently it fell to Vespasian's Legions and after that a Roman temple was built there. This was discovered during exploratory excavations. It is a unique experience to stand upon its wind-blown terraces and picture the desperate Early Britons fighting for their lives against the massively disciplined invaders from Rome. John Cowper Powys's romance *Maiden Castle*, though a modern story, convey's the atmosphere of haunted antiquity so characteristic of the place.

CERNE-ABBAS

Nestling beside the A352 about seven miles north of Dorchester, and in the valley of the River Cerne is Cerne Abbas which takes its name from the ruined abbey which was once so important in that part of the countryside.

D

Far older and much more famous than the abbey, however, is the Cerne Giant, carved out of the chalk downland on Trendle Hill, high above the village. This figure of a naked man bearing a club is some 180 feet long and it is thought by most antiquaries to be a representation of Roman Hercules, and that it originated, most probably in ancient fertility rites. Some think the figure is a combination representation of some early British god with the Roman Hercules attributes added. Certainly its monstrous proportions and bold affirmation of the life-urge dominate the landscape, and one can only marvel that it has survived so well through the centuries, even during the high tide of Puritanism in this country, when so many pagan representations were considered an affront by the godly!

Church of St. Mary

The church is of mainly fifteenth-century work save for its Norman chancel, and there is a fine screen and also some fourteenth- and fifteenth-century wall paintings. In a niche on the west side of the tower is an effigy of the Virgin Mary and Child. The village itself is very attractive with some Tudor and several Georgian houses, while not far from the church stands St. Augustine's Well, which was said to have been created miraculously by that saint.

Cerne Abbey

The ruins of the former abbey stand beyond the Abbey House; the Gateway and part of the Guest House are all that is left of the very fine monastery founded in 987 in memory of Edward the Martyr who had been murdered by the Danes a century earlier. In 1471 the warlike Lancastrian Queen, Margaret of Anjou, sought refuge there after her landing at Weymouth. She was no very pious lodger as she planned her warlike campaign against the Yorkists for the sake of her son's claim to the throne. She was destined to be brought to battle at Tewkesbury in Gloucestershire and there defeated. Her young son the Prince of Wales, son of Henry VI, was murdered before her eyes, and the Lancastrian cause seemed lost forever. The Abbey House is seventeenth century and the former great Tithe Barn of the abbey has been converted to private use.

The Cross-in-Hand

Beside a road that runs westward over the downland from High Stoy Hill there is a worn monolith standing completely isolated a few feet from the track. In his poem *The Lost Pyx* Hardy tells of the legend that this stone marked a spot where a former Abbot of Cerne had lost the pyx or metal box holding the holy wafer which he was taking to give the last rites to a dying labourer.

As he retraced his steps he saw a strange glow from Heaven illuminating the spot where the pyx lay and round it knelt all the wild and usually incompatible creatures of the fields and hedgerows, miraculously unafraid. All about the scene the air was as though charmed, despite the gales that raged over High Stoy Hill and the lanes round about. Therefore the Abbot knelt with the creatures of the woods and resolved to commemorate this event, which he did with the Cross-in-Hand. However there is a gipsy tradition that the pillar is a wishing stone.

Hardy described this village under the name of Abbot's Cernel in his Wessex books.

MINTERNE MAGNA

To the north of Cerne Abbas is the pretty village of Minterne Magna, set in the countryside of Hardy's *The Woodlanders*. At Minterne House there is a glorious wild shrub garden with magnificent rhododendrons, azaleas and magnolias. The Gardens are open, usually, on Sundays between April and June.

Just north of the village is High Stoy Hill which, at 846 feet affords splendid views over the Blackmoor Vale and westward towards Sherborne and Yeovil. On clear days the view is even more extensive and it is easy to call to mind Hardy's aristocratic young doctor, Edred Fitzpiers in *The Woodlanders*, whose habit it was to climb to a point on High Stoy and gaze out towards the home of the lady with whom he had become infatuated.

MAIDEN NEWTON

This pleasant little Dorset town is situated in the valley of the River Frome about seven miles north-west of Dorchester. The church is Norman in origin though only the tower remains, the rest of the building dating from the thirteenth and fourteenth centuries. The pleasant old inn, the 'White Horse' is a handsome building and there are many picturesque houses. The chapel dates from the eighteenth century.

BRIDPORT

Population: 6,500
Early Closing Day: Thursday
Market Days: Wednesday/Thursday

BRIDPORT IS AN ATTRACTIVE TOWN distinguished by wide streets and broad pavements. This is, to some extent, the legacy of its Georgian heyday and indeed it is still today one of the most important centres in this part of the west country. It is a good centre for holiday excursions and the seaside is only a mile to the south at West Bay. Thomas Hardy called it Port Bredy.

The town has a quite ancient history having been a Roman and later a Saxon settlement area, becoming in Edward the Confessor's time a mint town. Henry III granted Bridport a Borough charter and the town prospered, being famous among other things for rope-making. Fluctuation of fortune occurred during the Civil War, but evidently Charles II had a narrow escape from capture here in 1651 and thereafter remembered the place kindly, for when he 'came into his own again' he granted Bridport a further charter. An inscribed stone at the end of Lee Lane, east of the town, commemorates this lucky escape.

Monmouth's Rebellion

Bridport was again a centre of drama at the time of the young Duke of Monmouth's abortive rising against the Catholic king, James II, his uncle. Twelve of the Duke's wretched followers, simple countrymen for the most part, were found guilty of rebellion and hanged by the notorious 'Bloody Jeffreys' who held one of his merciless Assize Courts in Bridport. In the reign of George III it became a garrison town with its own barracks to house troops meant to beat off any possible invasion by French forces.

A Parvise

The parish church in Bridport is mainly Perpendicular, cruciform in shape and dominated by a fine central tower. Built in 1350 on the site of an earlier building, parts of the transepts are Early English in style. There was a good deal of Victorian restoration work carried out and and at the same time two bays were added to the nave. In 1924 the bells, eight in number, were recast and again restored to the tower where a chiming clock was also installed. The south porch boasts a room, or parvise, above it as well as a niche on the south side which may once have contained a shrine.

Historical Paintings

In South Street are the Daniel Taylor Almshouses. They house ten old people and were built in 1696. At the top of the same street is the Town Hall, an eighteenth-century building which has among its treasures a collection of paintings by a local artist recording historic episodes in the life of the town. It is a collection which may be viewed by the public subject to prior written application having been made to the Borough Offices at number 32, South Street. Among the ancient records kept at the Town Hall there is a will dating from 1268.

The Chantry

The most historic of the buildings in South Street is The Chantry so named because it is thought to have been the residence of the Prior of Bridport Abbey. Today it is the official Museum and houses some interesting exhibits. A remarkable one is that commemorating fifty years or so of rope-making, the major local industry, with examples of old nets, ropes and drying-lines. There are also some first-rate natural history collections, particularly British birds and their eggs.

The Roman relics are fascinating, especially the sheath of a Roman dagger, one of those items which touch a spring in the imagination, making real the dusty pages of far-off history. What hand once wielded that dagger? Was it some ordinary soldier, a homesick legionary, weary of our foggy, sea-girt land, and pining for his sunny Alban Hills, or was it an eager young military governor, making a name for himself in the far-flung Roman Empire?

Cider-making

North of Bridport is the village of Bradpole, a pleasant place with a Victorian church built in 1860 on the site of an earlier structure. Among its treasures is a sixteenth-century communion cup. In the nearby village of Loders the Church of St. Mary Magdalene is mainly in Perpendicular style though it retains a Norman doorway and window. The interior is attractive. There are a number of delightful cottages which add to the charm of the village.

Once upon a time Loders had a Benedictine Priory, founded in the reign of Henry I by one Baldwin de Redvers. Another Redvers granted this property to the Abbey of Coutances in Normandy and there is a strong tradition that monks of Coutances brought to England the recipe for cider-making which was to become so strongly associated with England and the West Country in particular.

West Bay

The little resort of West Bay is fast becoming popular and now has holiday homes close to its shingle beach, where bathing is possible. It is set at the mouth of the River Brit which is tidal, although no longer navigable as far as Bridport. The resort centres round the small harbour set between the cliffs, and boasts a small Esplanade. The original name of the place was Bridport Quay, or Bridport Harbour.

EYPE

Eype is the next little resort along the coast, westward from West Bay. The village straggles on beside the small Eype Brook, and centres round the church. This is the sort of place which attracts the more selective visitor who relishes peace and quiet. There is downland and cliff scenery in the neighbourhood, offering great contrasts of beauty while further west lies Eype Down (500 feet), on which there is a prehistoric earthwork of some interest. The continuation of this Down becomes Thorncombe Beacon (507 feet), beyond which lies Seatown at the mouth of the River Chid.

Link with Addison

Symondsbury lies a mile north from Eype and a mile west out of Bridport. It is a charming place set in a wooded hollow. The church,

mainly Perpendicular, has a tapering tower. Bishop Galston of Bristol
lies buried in this church; he was an uncle of Joseph Addison, the
writer and essayist who, with Richard Steele, edited *The Spectator*
among other magazines, and was noted for the purity and elegance
of his English. The local inn, called the Ilchester Arms, is a picturesque
place with a thatched roof. The conically shaped Colmer's Hill to
the west of Symondsbury is on the other side of Allington Hill.

CHIDEOCK

   Chideock is about three miles westward out of Bridport on the
A35. Its chief charm lies in the attractive aspect of the village and its
church which is Perpendicular in style and has some interesting
monuments. There was a fairly comprehensive programme of Victorian
restoration work in 1884. Of interest inside is the tomb of one of the
heroes of the Normandy wars of 1514 when he gained his
knighthood. Eventually, Sir John Arundel became lord of the manor
of Wardour in Wiltshire. The manor house has its own Roman
Catholic Chapel. To the south-west is Golden Cap with glorious cliff
scenery.

Chideock Church

St. Candida

   Whitchurch Canonicorum is on the southern side of Marshwood
Vale, watered by the River Char. The church is dedicated to St.
Candida and is cruciform, built in the transitional Norman manner,
parts of which remain today. There is a window which belongs to
the Perpendicular period. Within is the thirteenth-century shrine of
St. Candida, one of two in England (the other is that of Edward the

Confessor), of pre-Reformation date. Note the gargoyles which decorate the porch and the carvings on the tower, which may indicate that they are relics from the earlier, Saxon edifice.

Lambert's Castle

This prehistoric British earthwork is situated on the other side of Marshwood Vale, to the north-west of Whitchurch Canonicorum. It is set on a hill 841 feet high and thus affords a fine view over the surrounding countryside. It is said that it is named after the Danish ruler King Canute who became a Christian when he was King of England and adopted the baptismal name of Lambert. Two other excellent viewing points in the area are Castle Hill and Coneygar Hill.

BURTON BRADSTOCK

Burton Bradstock is set on the little River Bride, a mile and a half east of West Bay and very close to the sea. The name comes from 'Brideton Bradenstock,' this latter being the name of the Abbey in Wiltshire to which the property belonged. The Perpendicular style church is graced by a clock which came from old Christ's Hospital in London.

Beacon Knap

Bothenhampton, between Bridport and Burton Bradstock, has a church with a font dating from the eleventh century. Swyre, three miles to the east, has a church built originally in 1505 but much restored in the 1860's. West of Swyre is Beacon Knap (433 feet) and to the east is Puncknowle Hill (593 feet). Puncknowle is pretty and its manor house belonged to the Napier family. Chilcombe is another attractive village lying two miles to the north of Swyre, and north of the River Bride. West Bexington is a new resort on the coast standing one mile south-east of Swyre, near the sea.

BEAMINSTER

Set in the Dorset Downs about six miles north of Bridport, Beaminster is a most attractive country town. It is very old and at one time the manor belonged to Salisbury Cathedral, but there were three disastrous fires, two in the seventeenth century and one in the eighteenth, so that Beaminster has no very old buildings, save for the church with its monuments to the Strode family.

The main body of the church is fifteenth-century and there is a highly decorative Tudor tower. Built on the site of an earlier structure, there are recognisable portions of previous styles within the existing building.

The market cross in the square marks the centre from which the streets radiate and near the church is the historic Almshouse built by Sir John Strode in 1630, on the site of a former Chantry House.

Chief Justice

There are a number of very attractive villages around Beaminster. Two miles eastward is Mapperton which boasts an interesting manor house with both Tudor and Jacobean style architecture, though only one wing now remains. Netherbury and Melplash are two other pretty places to the south of the town. Stoke Abbot, three miles west of Beaminster once had the poet Crowe as its rector. Pilsdon, lying about two miles further west was the birthplace of Sir John Hody, who was Chief Justice of the King's Bench in 1440. Broadwindsor, about three miles slightly north-west of Beaminster, had for a rector, in the seventeenth century, Thomas Fuller, author of *English Worthies,* one of those books written with scholarly enthusiasm about notable people which has become, in its own right, one of the classics of our language.

Royal Escape

It was at Broadwindsor, too, that Charles II found refuge after having fled from Bridport in 1651. Here he lodged at the George Inn, where a plaque records this romantic and historic fact. This was just prior to his flight along the south coast eastward to Shoreham in Sussex, whence he escaped to France.

LYME REGIS

Population: 3,400
Early Closing Day: Thursday
Tourist Information Centre: (R) Boat House, Marine Parade
(Summer only)

ALONE AMONG THE SOUTH COAST RESORTS OF DORSET, Lyme Regis has managed to preserve and retain most of the grace and charm of its Regency heyday. Its narrow streets rise up from the quayside, where the unique, solidly built Cobb, or stone pier, guards the western side of the beautiful Lyme Regis Bay.

Royal Charter

The history of the resort is ancient indeed, having been granted its first charter by the King of Wessex in the eighth century. It was then assigned to Sherborne Abbey but was later transferred to the jurisdiction of the diocese of Salisbury. This was ceded to King Edward I and that was when Regis became part of the name of the town.

'Battles Long Ago'

The town was soon granted the liberties of a port and a borough and at this time the famous Cobb, the town's stone pier and breakwater was built. In the reign of Edward III Lyme Regis was contributing ships and men to the Navy, and in 1588, the year of the Spanish Armada, Lyme Regis sent two ships to the fleet protecting England, when the Battle of Portland Bill began far out at sea, though within sight of the town. It was a ship out of Lyme Regis which brought back the news in 1591, of Sir Richard Grenville's last stand against fifteen Spanish galleons in his little ship the 'Revenge'.

Later History

In the Civil War, Lyme Regis, (like Poole in the east), stood for Parliament, being briskly anti-royalist, and it withstood a royalist siege from mid-April to mid-June in 1644. On a beach west of the Cobb, the 'Protestant Duke' landed in 1685, seeking to unseat his Catholic uncle, James II. The 'Rebellion' was a miserable failure, and Monmouth was defeated in neighbouring Somerset, at Sedgemoor. Three years later, in 1688, William of Orange landed at Lyme Regis with his army, and for the same purpose. He was successful and, James II having fled the country, the Dutch prince, who was married to James's eldest daughter, was offered the throne jointly with his wife.

The Watering Place

In the eighteenth century the fortunes of Lyme revived, following a temporary decline of its position as a port, the advent of larger ships having made it somewhat redundant since it could not provide suitable harbour or dock facilities. Now it was 'discovered' as a fashionable watering place by the beaux and belles of Beau Nash's little kingdom at Bath. After taking the waters at Bath, the ladies and gentlemen of the leisured middle and upper classes would seek the seaside air and Lyme Regis was a natural venue, being almost due south of Bath.

The town has still many of its fine Georgian houses and shops with bow-fronted, bottle-glass windows which proclaim their origin as having been in the 'Age of Elegance'. The Marine Promenade, for pedestrians only, with its two-tier sun terraces and ornamental gardens is well-sheltered from the more noisy, traffic-burdened narrow streets of the main shopping area.

The Town Today

The beach at Lyme Regis is somewhat stony, and Bridge Street runs parallel with it where the River Lim enters the sea, and two main streets, Broad Street to the west, and Church Street in the east, wind up the hillside out of the main road.

In Bridge Street stands the Town Hall, late Victorian in construction but standing upon the site of the much older Guildhall. Here is held each month the 'Court of Hustings' as the Borough Council Meetings are called. Beneath it is the Old Market with an opening at the side leading to the Gun Cliff from which fine views may be obtained.

The Cobb

Book-lovers will know, of course, that much of the action of Jane Austen's novel, *Persuasion*, is set in Lyme Regis and it is related that when Lord Tennyson was visiting the resort and people tried to interest him in the beach where the reckless son of 'bold brown Lucy Walters', the Duke of Monmouth, landed with his troops, the poet said impatiently, 'Never mind Monmouth, show me where Louisa Musgrove fell!' He was referring to one of the major incidents in the novel, and though strictly speaking, the claims of historic reality ought to be superior, our best writers do have the power of imposing their fictional inventions upon any given topography to the exclusion of other interesting facts.

The Philpot Museum

Of special interest is the local Museum with its old prints, coins and historic documents and even a fire-engine dating from 1710. Particularly featured are many relics of the Monmouth Rebellion, and there are interesting volumes and documents in the neighbouring Library. Close by is the Buddle Bridge with arches dating from the fourteenth century.

Parish Church

The church of St. Michael the Archangel is unusual. The original Norman structure had a tower set between nave and chancel, but the existing one was built more to the east of the old tower round about 1500. The result is that the former nave now forms the west porch. Note the handsome seventeenth-century oak lectern where is displayed a copy of the *Paraphrase of St. Luke's Gospel* by Erasmus, Dutch scholar, pupil and friend of Sir Thomas More. There is a tapestry on the north wall depicting a Tudor marriage, though it is uncertain whether it is that of Henry VII to Elizabeth of York, or that of his son, Prince Arthur to Catherine of Aragon, in 1501. There are several interesting monuments and the stained glass windows are mainly nineteenth-century.

Almshouses

Above the church stand the Tudbold Almshouses, the gift of one Thomas Tudbold in 1548, though rebuilt in 1867. The six Marder Almshouses, built at the charge of Captain Nicholas Marder in 1892, stand in narrow, and old Coombe Street.

Famous Natives

Among distinguished people born in Lyme Regis must be numbered Thomas Coram, friend of Handel, who founded the children's home in London, the Foundling Hospital; Sir George Somers, a buccaneering sea-captain who first claimed the 'remote Bermudas' for Britain, calling them Somers Islands, and Elizabeth Coade, of 'Coade-stone' fame. This stone was made in a factory at

Lambeth in London and proved to be the most durable stone ever made artificially. When the factory was closed in 1840 the secret of its formula was lost, though there are many samples of work executed still to be found in the capital. The famous South Bank Lion is in Coade Stone; figures adorning the Norwegian Embassy in Belgrave Square and the tomb of Captain Bligh in Lambeth Churchyard are other notable examples of its durability. Especially charming are the little figures of a schoolboy and girl which adorn the Fan Makers' Hall in the churchyard of St. Botolph's Bishopsgate.

Ancient Beam

The country around Lyme Regis is full of interest. At Uplyme, just over a mile to the north and over the border in Devon, there is an Early English and Perpendicular church, much restored in the 1850's. An old Hotel there has an oak beam said to be 1,000 years old and a quaint passage dating from the thirteenth century. Here cider was made. During the reign of Henry VIII when the Catholic church fell into disgrace, a priest conducted a secret Mass in the panelled dining-room. He was caught, however, and paid for his temerity by being hanged, drawn and quartered.

Combpyne

About three miles west of Lyme Regis is Combpyne in Devon, noted for its thirteenth-century church with its tower arch, leper squint, piscina and Early English lancet window. There is a very ancient tenor bell in the belfry. The famous Communion Cup belonging to the church is kept up at the Manor House. It is unusual in having toes to the feet, while the chalice and paten are Pre-Reformation. Trinity Hill, north of the village, affords excellent views over the Axe Valley.

Ancient Inns

Charmouth, about two miles east of Lyme Regis, is a very old place mentioned in Saxon documents and in Domesday Book. The Church of St. Andrew, erected on the site of an older church, was rebuilt and enlarged in 1836. Its most notable feature is the east window, the work of Christopher Webb.

The Queen's Arms Hotel was once the guest-house of Forde Abbey Here a doorway built by Thomas Chard, the last Abbot of Forde, has been discovered. The hotel boasts a Gothic window, fine ceilings, walls and fireplaces. Henry VIII's first queen, Catherine of Aragon stayed here, and so did the 'Merry Monarch', Charles II. The crest of Catherine of Aragon is still to be found in the plaster of the bedroom used by her.

The George Hotel used to be a coach staging post. From here there are several paths to the beach and on the cliffs many fossils may be picked up.

The eastern cliff is the celebrated Golden Cap.

Section 4 North Dorset and Salisbury

BLANDFORD FORUM

Population: 3,650
Early Closing Day: Wednesday
Market Day: Thursday

BLANDFORD FORUM LIES ON THE River Stour some fifteen miles
north-west of Bournemouth. It is a fine centre for exploring Cranborne
Chase to the north, and the Dorset Downs to the west.

The town became a borough with the right to hold a market in
1218, although it was not granted a charter until 1605. Left
untouched by the Wars of the Roses and the Civil War, most of the
town was destroyed by a disastrous fire in 1731. Rebuilding began
at once, the architects being John and William Bastard, and as a
result of this, the town presents a very uniform appearance.

The centre of Blandford is its market place, where will be found the
Corn Exchange with its portico and fine pillars.

The Parish Church has an 80-feet-high tower surmounted by a
cupola, and was begun in 1732, the year after the fire, on the site of
the church which was destroyed. There is a noticeable lack of
coloured glass, except in the chancel windows.

Two fine streets are East Street and Salisbury Street, well
proportioned and with matching houses. The six-arched bridge over
the Stour is also impressive.

The chief buildings which survived the fire are Ryves Almshouses
in Salisbury Street built in 1682, and the Old House in the Close,
built by a German, Dr. Sagitarry. Both are fine buildings given
additional prominence by their Georgian surroundings.

Blandford St. Mary

Blandford St. Mary, across the Stour, was also largely destroyed in the fire of 1731. The church here is fourteenth-century, with many later additions. Thomas Pitt, grandfather of Lord Chatham, the eighteenth-century statesman is buried here. Down House, a mile to the west, was their family home. Browne Willis, the antiquary, was born here in 1682. Bryanston School is situated nearby.

The Winterborne

Westward from Blandford is the source of the River Winterborne, a tributary of the Stour. Many of the villages along the valley of the Winterborne are prefaced with the name of the river: Winterborne Clenston, Winterborne Kingston, Winterborne Stickland, etc. Northward from the latter is the village of Turnworth; Hardy used to cycle here on occasion to read the lesson in St. Mary's Church. A most rewarding journey is to continue northwards from Turnworth to the top of Okeford Hill—a distance of just over a mile. The climb is not particularly severe, and those who take this trip for the first time are usually quite unprepared for the absolutely magnificent view which appears suddenly when the top is reached. There is a place where one can park a car, and enjoy the view.

Bulbarrow

Westward from Okeford Hill lies Bulbarrow, the second highest point in Dorset, and from its height of 902 feet also a magnificent view-point. Here there is a toposcope to aid identification of the landmarks over the neighbouring counties, for one can see north and westward into Somerset, and distant parts of Wiltshire. On exceptionally clear days it is possible to glimpse the Black Mountains of Wales.

There are several earthworks around Bulbarrow, and nearby are Rawlsbury Rings, an ancient British hill fort.

Milton Abbas

Lying south-east of Bulbarrow, Milton Abbas is interesting not only for its beauty but also as an early example of planning. Milton Abbey was founded as a Benedictine establishment in 933 A.D. and given the status of Abbey in 964. The Abbey Church was rebuilt after a fire in 1309 but was not completed until 1400, the Abbot's Hall being built in 1498.

After the Dissolution of the Monasteries in 1539, the Abbot's Hall was sold for £1,000, and has remained in private hands ever since.

In 1752 the estate was purchased by Joseph Damer, who became Lord Milton, Earl of Dorchester. Not only did he pull down many of the Abbey buildings, but completely demolished the existing village because they spoiled his view!

However, in its place he built the present-day showpiece model village of thatched-roof cottages set in a long, gently inclined spacious road. At the bottom of this incline is a museum containing a selection of brewery, agricultural and rural impedimenta from a bygone age.

Milton Abbey is now a public school which incorporates the original Abbot's Hall and is best viewed from the road which leads from the nearby village of Hilton.

Nearby is the fourteenth-century Abbey Church where there is a magnificent altar screen and many other interesting features. St. Catherine's Chapel in the adjacent woods dates from the 10th century. The grounds and the church are always open to the public, but other places only occasionally.

CRANBORNE CHASE

Once an extensive Forest, Cranborne Chase is an area of high chalk downs partly in Dorset and partly in Wiltshire.

The highest point entirely in Dorset is Ashmore Down, 810 feet, but this particular down has an eastern summit of 862 feet on the Wiltshire border. The highest point is a mile to the east and inside Wiltshire—Win Green, 911 feet above sea level.

While the forest has virtually disappeared, some fine woodlands may be seen in the area. The village of Tollard Royal is the centre for the Chase and King John's House and Rushmoor House both have historic associations. There is also an attractive thirteenth-century church.

Cranborne, which gave its name to the Chase, is situated on the Crane, some twelve miles east-north-east of Blandford. Hardy calls it Chaseborough, and the nearby Pentridge is referred to as Trantridge. Cranborne Abbey once came under Tewkesbury, but it vanished at the Dissolution: all that remains today is the church of St. Mary and St. Bartholomew, twelfth–thirteenth century, with a fourteenth-century tower containing eight bells.

STURMINSTER NEWTON

Population: 2,250
Early Closing Days: Wednesday and Saturday
Market Day: Monday

STURMINSTER NEWTON LIES IN THE Vale of Blackmoor, on the River Stour: the name derives from Stour Minster, 'minster' denoting its former connection with Glastonbury Abbey. The place was once divided into two parts, Sturminster to the north-east of the Stour and Newton, or New Town, to the south-west.

The bridge over the Stour is a fine example of medieval work; beside the river can be seen earthworks, which are all that is left of the old castle. The church on the river bank, about half-a-mile

downstream from the bridge has fourteenth-century stone work
and a fifteenth-century waggon-beam roof.

There is a pleasant little market square with many Georgian houses,
and a Victorian drinking fountain in the centre. The vicarage garden
in Church Street contains a never-failing spring.

A mile to the east, the water-mill at Fiddleford is worth a visit.

Sturminster Common

In Newton, on the other side of the Stour, there is a signpost
indicating the road to 'Broad Oak and Dirty Gate'. This leads to
Sturminster Common and Banbury Hill, 360 feet, where there is a
prehistoric earthwork, and from where views over the Blackmoor
Vale can be enjoyed.

Sturminster Newton has always been an important market centre.
A scheme for the insemination of cattle was devised in 1944, and
the buildings erected in 1947. In the following year a special and
separate attested and licensed T.T. sale yard for cattle was added.

Some four miles north of Sturminster Newton is Marnhull,
generally held to be the original of 'Marlott' in Hardy's novels, and
indeed was the birthplace of Tess in *Tess of the D'Urbervilles*. Its
two inns feature in the book also. The fine church here has a
pinnacled tower, and is Early English.

Yew Forest

Once called Shillingstone Okeford, this village takes its name
from the Eschellings, a Saxon tribe. The church is built from
material dating from various periods. There were once two inns called
the New Ox and the Old Ox, which points to the place having been
on a drovers' road. The Old Ox is now called the Good Earth.

Hambledon Hill, 622 feet, where can be found a 'forest' of yew
trees, lies north-west from Shillingstone.

SHAFTESBURY

Population: 4,000
Early Closing Day: Wednesday
Market Day: Thursday

SHAFTESBURY IS ONE OF THE FEW TOWNS in Britain to have
been built on a hill-top. There are, of course, fine views all around,
but especially to the north-west where, on a clear day, the Mendip
Hills can be seen.

Shaftesbury, the 'Shaston' of Hardy's novels, was known to the
Britons as Paladwr, or the Dark Fortress, and was important under
the Romans. It became the site of a large Abbey, founded by King
Alfred, in 888 A.D., which survived until the Dissolution of 1539.

Edward the Martyr, murdered at Corfe in 978, was re-interred in the Abbey in 981. King Canute died here in 1035.

The Earls of Shaftesbury, of whom several have played an important part in British politics, take their title from the town.

Byzant

There is a central square, and in the Town Hall, dominated by its clock, two maces are kept—one dates from 1475, the other from 1604. The official corporate seal of 1570, and the Byzant used to bring water to this hill-top can also be seen.

Close by is the Museum, and adjoining this, the Abbey ruins. Gold Hill is a steep, picturesque street, with the ancient town wall nearby.

St. Peter's Church is the oldest of the four surviving churches, and has a high tower visible for many miles around. It is mainly early fifteenth-century, the six bells in the tower are all inscribed, and the east window has some stained glass contemporary with the building of the church. There is a large crypt, once used as a beer cellar by the public house next door.

St. Rumbold's Church was mainly rebuilt in the nineteenth century, but has a Norman font. Holy Trinity has a mutilated effigy, probably from the Abbey, and St. James, in the south of the town has an interesting east window. These last two were also mainly rebuilt in the nineteenth century.

GILLINGHAM

Population: 4,100
Early Closing Day: Thursday

THE NAME OF THE TOWN IS PRONOUNCED with a hard 'G' as in 'go', unlike its Kentish namesake which has a soft 'G' as in 'gentle'.

This place has been inhabited since prehistoric times, but the first important recorded event was a battle at Slaughter Green, to the west of the town, in 1016, when Edmund Ironside defeated the Danish King Canute.

In 1042, a Saxon parliament (Witanagemote) was held here, which led to the decision that Edward the Confessor should succeed to the throne of England. In those days Gillingham was surrounded by forests which were a royal domain, but these were removed in the reign of Charles I to make way for really fertile farming land.

Gillingham church, in the centre of the town, was built between 1276 and 1370. It was partially reconstructed in 1838, has a monument dated 1133, a thirteenth-century chancel, and a tomb from 1625.

SHERBORNE

Population: 8,750
Early Closing Day: Wednesday
Market Day: Thursday

SHERBORNE IS ONE OF THE MOST IMPORTANT places in the north of Dorset, and is famed for its Abbey Church, the cathedral of a diocese for three-and-a-half centuries. It has two castles, the older being mainly in ruins.

Sherborne grew up in early Saxon days, taking its name from the Scire Burn, or clear brook as that part of the River Yeo was then called.

Cathedral

A cathedral was completed in 705 A.D. and the western half of the unwieldy Winchester diocese was transferred to it, with St. Aldhelm as first bishop. Sherborne School was founded at the same time and, according to tradition, King Alfred was educated there.

Monastery

A Monastery grew up around the cathedral, and this remained when the see was removed to Old Sarum in 1072. At first the townsfolk used the Monastery Church as a parish church, and built Allhallows Church in the thirteenth century: disputes between the townsfolk and the monks led to the Abbey Church being set on fire and partially destroyed. The monks then yielded to the townsfolk who paid for the reconstruction of the church which was completed in 1490, and led to Pack Monday Fair, the second Monday in October being set aside for a fair to celebrate the packing up of the workmen's equipment.

The Castle

The castle was also the scene of stirring events. It was captured for King Stephen in 1139: Sir Walter Raleigh built much of the sixteenth-century structure, and later it was held for the Royalists in the Civil War, being twice besieged by the Roundheads.

In 1688 William of Orange spent a night here on his way to London, and his proclamation is said to have been printed in the New Castle; this was opened to the public in 1969.

Abbey Church

The Abbey Church is mostly Perpendicular in style, but there is Norman work in the west end of the south side. The most striking feature of the whole building is the fan-vaulting on the roof of the Nave and the Choir. The Perpendicular windows are also very fine: note the designs on the bosses.

At the west end of the north aisle is a Saxon doorway, all that
E

remains of the Saxon church: this was reopened and a porch built over it by the Friends of Sherborne Abbey in 1947, as a thank-offering for the survival of the Abbey during the Second World War.

Link with Wolsey

At the eastern end of the south aisle is the Leweston, or St. Katherine's Chapel, containing the tomb of John Leweston (died 1584). A fine oak roof covers the south transept, where there are memorials to the Digby family, and a fine east window.

The carving on the monks' stalls in the choir matches the lovely fan-vaulting on the roof.

The tower may be climbed: the tenor bell here was presented by Cardinal Wolsey, who was at one time tutor to the son of the Marquis of Dorset.

Near the Abbey are the picturesque Almshouses founded in 1437 for twenty old men and women. The buildings were extended in 1858 and 1866.

Sherborne Schools

North of the Abbey is Sherborne School, founded in 705 by St. Aldhelm and refounded as a grammar school in 1550 by Edward VI. The old monastery buildings have been converted for school use. Other schools are Sherborne School for Girls, Fosters School, founded in 1640, and Lord Digby's School for Girls.

King's Refuge

Trent, three miles north-west of Sherborne, has a manor house where Charles II hid for several weeks in 1651, before escaping across the Channel by ship. The owner of the manor was Colonel Wyndham, who lies buried in the church.

SALISBURY

Population: 36,000
Early Closing Day: Wednesday
Market Days: Tuesday and Wednesday
Tourist Information Centre: (N) 10 Endless Street

SALISBURY IS FAMOUS FOR ITS CATHEDRAL, which has the tallest spire in England, soaring to a height of 404 feet. The cathedral itself is a magnificent building in an idyllic setting, and the city is bustling and clean, and has many old streets and houses.

Old Sarum

The original settlement was at Old Sarum, some two miles north of the present city, the first inhabitants arrived in the Iron Age and built the earthworks, probably an important fortress, which survive to this day.

The Romans called the place Sorbiodunum and made it a strong military centre, capable of holding down this new portion of their empire, although with the pacification of southern Britain it is likely that it became more of a commercial than a military centre. After the departure of the Romans, the Saxons, under Cynric captured Sorbiodunum, renaming it Searobyrg: it later grew in importance, and, for a time, was the capital of Wessex.

Alfred the Great strengthened the castle and, despite being razed to the ground in the eleventh century, the place resumed growth after being rebuilt by the Normans, who founded a cathedral: this was damaged in a fierce storm within a few days of its completion, but was immediately repaired. The work was carried out by Osmond, the second Bishop of Salisbury, who compiled a missal on which was based the *Sarum Use*. The *Sarum Breviary* was printed in 1483, in Venice, and became the foundation of the liturgy in the English prayer books of Edward VI.

New Town

There was continual friction between the garrison and the clergy because of the limited space available, and in 1217 the Dean and Chapter successfully petitioned the Pope Honorius III for a licence

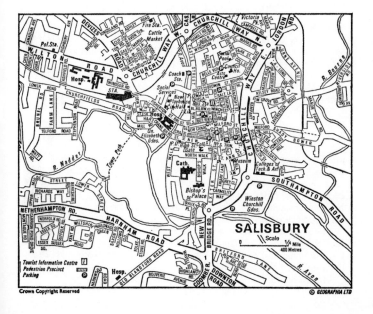

to move to the more fertile site in the valley. Work on the new cathedral and the new city began in 1220, and in 1227 Henry III granted the city its first charter. Nine further charters were granted, the earliest in 1270, and the latest in 1707. The population began to drift down to the new city, and Old Sarum gradually became a dead place and its walls were demolished in 1608. Nevertheless, it continued to send two Members to Parliament until 1832.

New Sarum
The new city began to grow and thrive and was built on a gridiron pattern with its streets at right angles to one another. It rapidly became a thriving market centre and in 1612 the charter granted by James I permitted Salisbury to be called the city of New Sarum, and to have a Mayor.

The Civil War
There was no actual fighting in the immediate neighbourhood of Salisbury during the Civil War, although the city was a halting-place for both sides in the preliminary manoeuvring before the Second Battle of Newbury in 1644, and the Battle of Langport in 1645.

The Salisbury of the nineteenth century began to expand rapidly in size and was fortunately untouched by the First World War, although in the Second a little bombing was experienced. In 1954 the boundries of the city were extended to include Old Sarum so that after more than seven centuries the two cities were united.

The Cathedral
Salisbury Cathedral followed after that erected in Old Sarum, and which was so beautiful a place that William of Malmesbury said of it: 'Lord, I have loved the glory of Thy house'.

Old Sarum Cathedral has a worthy successor: the foundations were laid in 1220 and the building completed in 1258. The cathedral was consecrated in that year, and dedicated in 1260.

This very fine example of Early English architecture survived unscathed for many centuries, even during the Civil War, but great harm was done to it in 1790, when the stained glass was taken out, and screens and other adornments were removed by the architect Wyatt, known as 'The Destroyer', who was 'restoring' the cathedral. Even the walls were whitewashed, and although this was cleaned off before very long, the interior seems austere because of the lack of coloured glass windows. It is, nonetheless, impressive because the whole length of the cathedral can be seen, as there is no screen or organ to impede the view.

The nave is divided into ten arches, the top of the vaulting is 81 feet above floor level. The pillars supporting it are of Purbeck marble, but the walls and the ribs of the vaulting are of freestone from the Chilmark Quarries near Salisbury.

The cathedral has a double set of transepts, those on the

north-west and south-west. In the 'restoration' of 1790, tombs which had hitherto been scattered about the cathedral were placed on the south side of the nave in the south aisle. These include the tombs of the two William Longswords, father and son, an unknown bishop of the thirteenth century, and St. Osmond, builder of the cathedral.

In the chapel of St. Michael, leading off the south-east transept, is the memorial to the dead of the First World War: those of the Second World War are commemorated in two windows by the north door.

Spire Supports

Features of interest include the works of the clock which dates from 1386 and is the oldest piece of mechanism in Great Britain still in good working order. Note also the supports in the nave for the spire which was added to the original building without the construction of any extra foundation; consequently strengthening has been needed throughout the life of the cathedral.

The west front is also worthy of note, as it has a large number of niches which hold the figures of saints.

The Library

To the west of the cathedral are the fine cloisters, and the octagonal Chapter House, in Early Decorated style, which was added in 1280.

The Library, situated to the east of the Cloisters, contains many treasures, including one of the manuscripts of Magna Carta, signed at Runnymede in 1215, brought to Old Sarum and kept in the cathedral there. It was transferred to the new cathedral, where it remained from 1225 until 1940, when it was hidden, for safety, in a quarry during the Second World War: it was returned to the cathedral in 1945.

The earliest manuscripts in the library are from the eighth century: other treasures include the tenth-century *Sarum Psalter* and the beautifully illustrated *Sarum Breviary* of 1440.

Mompesson House

The cathedral, in its Close, has no obstructing building nearby except for the Bishop's Palace, the earliest parts of which date from the thirteenth century. The building is now in use as the cathedral school, sixteen choristers being among the pupils.

Other points of interest in the Close are the Exeter Gate leading to the Bishop's Palace, Mompesson House, which belonged to the merchant family of Mompesson, has a carved staircase, good plaster and woodwork and now belongs to the National Trust, and St. Ann's Gate leading on to St. Ann Street. Here is the Salisbury, South Wilts and Blackmore Museum which houses an historical collection going back to prehistoric times. Nearby is the former Joiners' Hall, now two houses.

Market Place

In St. John Street, running north from St. Ann's Gate, is the White Hart Hotel. Continuing, the road becomes Catherine Street, then Queen Street before running into the Market Place. No. 8, Queen Street, known as the House of John A'Port, was built in 1425.

The chief building on the Market Place is the Guildhall, dating from 1795. The Poultry Cross, mentioned as early as 1335 and scheduled as an Ancient Monument, is situated in the south-west corner.

Salt Lane, north of the Market Place, contains the fine Shoemakers' Guildhall, and has, next to it, a fine timber-framed old house. In Clipper Lane, a westward continuation of Salt Lane is the Public Library. The Haunch of Venison Inn stands on Silver Street, south-west of the Market Place.

The church of St. Thomas of Canterbury, in Perpendicular style, and restored in 1868, stands to the west of Market Place. North-east of Market Place is Bourne Hill, site of the Council House, formerly the College of St. Edmund which was taken over by the city in 1927 to celebrate the seven hundredth anniversary of the original charter of New Sarum.

WILTON

Population: 4,000
Early Closing Day: Wednesday

ONCE THE COUNTY TOWN OF WILTSHIRE and claiming to be the third oldest borough in England, Wilton lies three miles west of Salisbury on the A30.

Wilton House, which is open to the public, is the home of the

Wilton House

Earl of Pembroke, and was built on the site of a Benedictine abbey by Inigo Jones and Wyatt: it houses a splendid collection of furniture and old paintings. A huge collection, over 7,000, of model soldiers of the nineteenth century can be seen.

Sidney and Shakespeare

The earlier Elizabethan house was the home of Mary Sidney, wife of the second Earl of Pembroke. Here she surrounded herself with great artists and writers: her brother, Sir Philip Sidney, and Shakespeare himself, visited Wilton. The house they knew was, unhappily, damaged disastrously by a fire in 1647.

Royal Carpet Factory

The Wilton Royal Carpet Factory can also be visited. This, the oldest carpet factory in England, occupies a mixture of eighteenth- and twentieth-century buildings.

Wilton church was built in 1848 in the Byzantine style, unusual in Great Britain. The campanile is 108 feet high.

Regimental Badges

At Fovant, seven miles west of Wilton, there are regimental badges which were cut into the chalk hillside by troops stationed there in the First World War. These lie to the south of the A30: a drum-head service is held here each June, attended by representatives of the regiments whose badges can be seen.

Nelson's Home

Two places worth visiting lie to the south of Salisbury, on the road to Fordingbridge and Bournemouth. Downton is on the Avon: go five miles along the Bournemouth road and it will be found not far from the boundary with Hampshire, and to the north-west of the New Forest. The ancient Moot at Downton was, perhaps, the meeting place of the Saxon Parliament.

The red-brick Trafalgar House, once the home of Lord Nelson, stands nearby.

Longford Castle

Longford Castle, an Elizabethan mansion in a fine park, and the home of the Earl of Radnor, lies three miles south-east of Salisbury: here, too, an attractive collection of pictures and furniture can be seen.

Longford Castle is set in beautiful wooded country, and the villages of Alderbury, East Grimstead and West Grimstead in the fine sylvan setting east of the castle are worth exploring.

To the south-east is the long Dean Hill, 512 feet. This is a good vantage point from where Salisbury in its hollow can be seen to the north-west, and far to the south-east the silver streak of Southampton Docks are quite visible. The main Salisbury-Southampton road crosses the Dean Hill ridge at Pepperbox Hill.

Section 5   New Forest and Hampshire Coast

THE NEW FOREST

THE NEW FOREST IS THE LARGEST AREA OF WOODLAND and open heath country in England and is 92,365 acres in extent. Originally it stretched from the Wiltshire border in the north to the south coast and from the Avon in the west to Southampton Water in the east. Down the centuries the area has been deforested and now, what is left nowhere reaches the Avon, although coming within less than a mile of it in the most north-westerly corner. Its northern boundary is still the Wiltshire border, but it no longer extends right to the coast in the south, save for a small section on the Solent east of Lymington.

The Conqueror

William I ordered the afforestation of the area which we now call the New Forest in 1079, and there were tales of hardships suffered by those who were displaced to make the king's hunting ground. The historical and geological evidence suggests that there was some exaggeration on this score as not only are there settlements in the area with buildings, mainly churches, of Norman or pre-Norman origin, but the soil was never anything but poor and so probably never did support a flourishing farming community. Indeed, nature had already begun the work which The Conqueror merely continued when he created his New Forest.

Ships for the Navy

The boundaries of the New Forest were reduced gradually. This began in the reign of Edward I in the thirteenth century, and by the reign of Charles II in the seventeenth century they were much as they are today. New Forest trees were felled to make ships for the Navy—England's famous 'wooden walls', but there was a good deal of timber-stealing, and in time the trees left for the naval ships were inferior and a shortage of wood seemed likely.

Timber Stealing

The first re-afforestation was begun in 1669, by order of Charles II, four hundred acres being enclosed for the growing of oak trees. A further six thousand acres were planted in the reign of William III (1698), but in 1703 a tremendous gale uprooted so many trees as to undo much of the good work that had been done in making new plantations. During the next century timber-stealing again became prevalent and despite a new method of planting, begun in 1808, there was little improvement in matters until the appointment of a Commission on the New Forest. After that the New Forest was administered much more efficiently until in 1928 it was transferred to the care of the Foresty Commission. There was further Parliamentary action on the New Forest in 1968.

Varied Scenery

The New Forest is, on the whole, open to all, and this includes the enclosures which are kept in good order. These are where the young trees for re-afforestation schemes are planted. The scenery varies enormously, heathy ground with the prevailing yellow soil alternates with woodland glades and open areas of grass, interspersed with streams, ponds and leafy walks. Much of the Forest is dominated by the scent of gorse, the humming of hundreds of insects and the songs of the wild birds. This is the ideal place for naturalists, botanists and all who love the woodlands, while its true beauty is best explored on foot, for even a bicycle or car limit full exploration of the lonelier glades, and the more secluded rides. Horseback, of course, is the ideal means by which to get to know this fine Forest.

Fine Old Trees

The commonest trees in the New Forest are oak, ash, beech, chestnut, larch, Scots pine and Douglas fir—the last named being a favourite for planting because of its rapid growth. There are few elms, but other fairly common trees are alder, birch, holly, lime, maple and willow. In Knightswood is Tallest Oak, 22 feet across at a point some four feet above the ground, while near Moyles Court there is a slightly smaller oak which is nevertheless 20 feet and 4 inches in diameter at only four feet above the ground. Other famous trees are The Queen's Bower Oak, the Twin Beeches in Bramshaw Wood and a single beech in Vinney Ridge; all are remarkable for their size.

Forest 'Walks'

As well as having scheduled Nature Reserves, the New Forest is divided into 'Walks', each with its own keeper or forester to look after the area alloted. Many of these Walks are very ancient and the whole Forest is administered by means of the Deputy Surveyor and the Verderers' Court which sits five times a year at Lyndhurst. It is the only surviving office attached to the Forest and tries offences against the laws of the forest. Grazing rights have to be paid for as do turbary rights (digging peat on land belonging to another), pannage (the right to turn the pig herd out to eat acorns in autumn), and smoke money (the right of turf-cutting). These particular rights belong to the 'hearth' or messuage, and not to the individual landlord or tenant. Agisters, or marksmen check that the Forest animals have been marked and help to round up the ponies.

The Fauna

Apart from the famous ponies, descendants of the jennets, or light Spanish horses which swam ashore from the wrecked ships of the Armada in 1588, the New Forest is rich in fauna.

There are three species of deer in the Forest—the red, the roe and the fallow deer. Other forest creatures are badgers, foxes, hares, otters, rabbits, squirrels, stoats and weasels. The red squirrel is now extinct and only the grey is in evidence. There is, in addition, a wide variety of species among birds and insects as well as a great variety of wild flowers, lichens and fungi.

Rivers

The main rivers of the New Forest are the Lymington and the Beaulieu. Both rise within the Forest and flow south-eastwards to empty into the Solent, and both have estuaries. That of the River Lymington is only a small one, but the estuary of the River Beaulieu is over four miles long. There are several fine ponds in the Forest, and also interesting archaeological relics.

LYNDHURST

Population: 2,500
Early Closing Day: Wednesday
Forestry Commission Information Centre: Public Car Park, High
Street (summer only)

LYNDHURST, SET AMIDST ONE OF THE LOVELIEST AREAS of the New Forest, is often called the 'capital' of the area. Its name derives from the lime, or linden wood, and the town appears in Domesday Book as Linhest.

It is a pretty place with a church which dominates the town and very attractive surroundings enhance the 'village' aspect of the place. Nearby is Knightswood with Tallest Oak, and also Mark Ash Wood with its handsome beeches.

The Church of St. Michael and All Angels replaced an eighteenth-century structure. It is entirely nineteenth-century but is embellished with ornamentation by Burne-Jones, Millais and Lord Leighton. It is noted for the fresco in the chancel, delineating the Parable of the 'wise' and the 'foolish' Virgins painted by Hamilton Aide and presented by his friend, Lord Leighton. The corbel heads adorning the church represent martyrs and reformers connected with the church, and in the attractive churchyard lies the original 'Alice' of *Alice in Wonderland*. Mrs. Alice Hargreaves, née Liddell, who with her little sisters, was much loved by Lewis Carroll in his Oxford days.

Forest Court

Nearby is Queen's House with its ivied walls, once the home of the Lord Warden of the Forest. It is now a private residence save for the wing which houses the offices of the Deputy Surveyor. One of these is the Verderers' Hall and Court Room where meetings are held to transact business or deal with offences against the Forest laws. The prisoner's dock has been carved by an axe while among the antlers displayed on the otherwise bare walls are a pair locked together as a result of a fight between stags. An old stirrup measuring $10\frac{1}{2}$ inches by $7\frac{1}{2}$ inches was used for measuring dogs, as only those who could pass through it were allowed into the Forest.

Foxlease Hall

Other buildings of interest are the Crown Inn, which is Tudor style, though rebuilt about 1897, and the Lyndhurst Park Hotel, formerly a private house. One of its former tenants was Admiral Sir Arthur Philip, the first Governor of Australia. Foxlease Hall to the south of the town belongs to the Girl Guides Association, having been donated by an American lady, Mrs. Archibald, in 1922.

Sir John Barleycorn

At Cadnam about three and a half miles north of Lyndhurst on the boundary of the New Forest, there is a pleasant old inn called the Sir John Barleycorn, and also some attractive cottages. At Minstead, an unspoiled village about half a mile west there is a church which in appearance resembles a group of cottages. Among its many features of interest, is a sloping, three-decker pulpit.

Rufus Stone

Half a mile north from Malwood and a mile south-west of Cadnam stands the Rufus Stone, marking the spot where William II was fatally wounded by an arrow discharged from the bow of Sir Walter Tyrrell on August 2nd, 1100. The stone was erected in 1745 by the

Earl de la Warr but by 1841 it was found necessary to cover the stone with iron as a protection against name-carvers.

North of the Rufus Stone and west of Cadnam are the villages of Brook and Bramshaw. Bramshaw Golf Course is, actually, at Brook despite the name. The church and churchyard of Bramshaw are worth a visit, while to the west lies Bramble Hill (414 feet), affording glorious views, as also does Bramshaw Telegraph Post Hill (419 feet), and the very summit of the New Forest. This latter is, in fact, only a few yards from the county and the Forest boundary, although the heathy and wooded terrain extends a further mile or two into the south-east corner of Wiltshire.

Fritham

Southwards the fine expanse of heath and woods slopes gently to the Avon valley. Fritham, a mile south of the county boundary is very old in its origins. There are extensive remains of prehistoric inhabitants all over the district. It was to Fritham that William Rufus was carried after his injury from Sir Walter Tyrrell's arrow and here, indeed, the king died. Nearly nine centuries later historians are arguing still as to whether that death was 'accidental' or not!

Shy Deer

Along Bolderwood Walk, about two miles to the west of Lyndhurst, one can more readily see the deer, though they are still very wary and shy of people. South of Lyndhurst, on either side of the road to Brockenhurst is the extensive area of the forest known as the Irons Hill Walk.

BEAULIEU

Population: 1,500
Early Closing Day: Tuesday
Tourist Information Centre: (L) National Motor Museum

BEAULIEU IS AN UNSPOILED VILLAGE situated on the river of the same name at the point where it becomes tidal. It is dominated by the ruins of its Abbey which was founded in 1204 by King John after he had suffered terrifying dreams about the Last Judgement. It was a Cistercian foundation and lasted until the Dissolution of the Monasteries in 1539 when most of the buildings were either damaged or destroyed. The manor had been sold the previous year to Thomas Wriothesley who became Earl of Southampton. Then it passed by marriage to first the Montagus and then the Buccleuch families. It was given in 1865 by the fifth Duke of Buccleuch as a wedding present to his son, Lord Henry Scott who was created first Baron Montagu of Beaulieu in 1885. He and his son, the second

Baron, did much to preserve and restore the Abbey ruins. The present Lord Montagu founded the Motor Museum in 1952 in memory of his father, a pioneer in the field of motoring.

The Abbey

Enough remains of the Abbey to enable the visitor to picture what must once have been a magnificent foundation. The Great Gatehouse, outside the main ruins, is Palace House, today part of the home of Lord Montagu, while the Cloisters and the Chapter House were restored through the efforts of the first two barons both of whom have been buried there. The Domus Conversorum was restored in 1909 and made into a hall and the Cellarers' building below is now a café. The former lay brothers Refectory is now a museum.

The church of the Abbey was pulled down after the Dissolution and what was once the Monk's Refectory has become the parish church of Beaulieu. It is unusual in that it runs north to south. To the north of the Abbey are the remains of the old Winepress and a neighbouring field still bears the name of 'the Vineyards'.

The Motor Museum

The National Motor Museum in the grounds of Palace House has one of the world's finest collections of old and interesting road vehicles. Not only cars, but trams, motor-cycles and bicycles are to be seen, as well. Of unique interest is the Spitfire Fighter plane once used by Air Chief Marshal Sir James Robb.

Exbury Gardens

Some three miles south-west of Beaulieu is the village of Exbury where the church contains fine bronze memorials to the Forster family, killed during the First World War. In the spring there is a splendid show of flowers and shrubs at Exbury Gardens, an estate of some 250 acres. Open from April to June the Gardens have a magnificent show of rhododendrons, azaleas, and camellias which should not be missed by any visitor to the area. Nearby is Lepe with views over the Solent to the Isle of Wight. This yachting centre has a small, stony beach and a country park for picnics, etc.

Beaulieu Heath

Opposite Exbury and south-west of the Beaulieu River estuary is Buckler's Hard, a pretty village leading down to the water's edge. It was an important shipbuilding centre in the days of the Navy's 'wooden walls' and one of the many battleships built here was the 46-gun *Agamemnon* of Nelson's fleet. Here is the Maritime Museum tracing the history of Buckler's Hard. A mile south of Buckler's Hard is St. Leonards, where the grange or granary, used by the monks of Beaulieu Abbey still stands, as does their chapel. A couple of miles further west and near the waters of the Solent is Sowley Pond.

Beaulieu Heath extends over a considerable distance on both sides

of Beaulieu and in this area, a mile west of the village, is Hatchet
Pond. The terrain here has been likened by some to the South African
veldt. Denny Lodge Inclosure, Frame Heath Inclosure, Hawkhill
Inclosure, Great Goswell Copse and Ashen Wood are among the
important woodlands in the vicinity of Beaulieu.

BROCKENHURST

Population: 3,000
Early Closing Day: Wednesday

BROCKENHURST LIES IN THE SOUTH of the New Forest. It is on
the main line from London and Southampton to Bournemouth. The
name means 'Badger's Wood'.
    The parish church is dedicated to St. Nicholas, is Norman and
Early English in style and stands on a mound which was probably
the site of an earlier church. Though there is Norman work to be
seen in the church most of the structure is Early English and there is
an interesting survival in the 'Squire's Pew'. In the church there is a
memorial to 101 New Zealanders who gave their lives in the First
World War and their national flag marks it. They are buried outside
in the pleasant little churchyard where also is to be found the
memorial stone of a local 'character', Harry Mills, better known as
'Brusher' Mills, who lived alone in a forest hut, and was an official
snake-catcher in the New Forest. The stone mentions that he
became an object of interest to many because of his primitive way
of life, which did not however, afford him any greater health than
others for he died suddenly, aged 67.
    Other interesting graves are those of Mary Axford who lived to be
101 years old, and that of the local schoolmistress, Mary Ann Ash,
who taught for over fifty years and whose career is commemorated
in verse.

Unusual Collection

    Brockenhurst is a most attractive village and in its vicinity are some
of the gems of the area, notably Queen Bower Wood, and the
Ornamental Drive with its many rhododendrons and named specimens.
There is also New Park in the neighbourhood venue of the famous
Agricultural Show.
    There are a number of thatched cottages, and the Baptist Chapel
was built in 1692, though later considerably reconstructed; St.
Saviour's Church is purely twentieth-century. Brockenhurst Station,
the junction for Lymington, is of particular interest for the unusual
collection of signed photographs which adorn the walls of the
waiting-room on the down platform. They were presented by a Mrs.
Cameron to the then London and South Western Railway to celebrate

the fact that here she met one of her sons returning to England after a long time overseas. The collection includes photographs of Robert Browning, Alfred Lord Tennyson, the English poets, Henry Wadsworth Longfellow, the American poet; F. Watts the artist, and Bishop Wilberforce of Winchester.

Heath and Woodlands

South of Brockenhurst is Setley Plain, a pleasant heath with a couple of ponds and prehistoric earthworks. East of Brockenhurst there is a large area of woodland which can also be reached easily from Beaulieu. Frame Wood, about halfway between Brockenhurst and Beaulieu, is one of the oldest stretches of woodland in the New Forest. Three miles south-east of Brockenhurst is the village of Boldre, where the church is worth a visit. Nearby is rebuilt Heywood Manor, reconstructed from a ruin, in Gothic style, in 1903.

Riding Centre

West of Brockenhurst is a large tract of heathland known as Rhinefield Walk which slopes gently northward to the Ober Water. Half-way between Brockenhurst and Ringwood is Burley village, a noted riding and hunting centre. North of Burley and north-west of Brockenhurst there stretches a large area of the New Forest which is almost roadless and contains no villages. Much of the ground is open heath, though there are many woodland expanses too, the most important being Roe Wood Inclosure, Broomy Inclosure, and Amberwood Inclosure. Hale Purlieu, just inside Hampshire, but just beyond the official area of the New Forest, is an attractive expanse of heath belonging to the National Trust.

LYMINGTON

Population: 6,600
Early Closing Day: Wednesday
Market Day: Saturday

LYMINGTON IS SITUATED JUST OUTSIDE the New Forest and at the mouth of the River Lymington. It is the terminus of the branch line from Brockenhurst and the place from which British Rail steamers sail for Yarmouth in the Isle of Wight, carrying cars as well as passengers. It is an attractive little town with places like Milton, Barton-on-Sea, Hordle, Sway, Pennington and Milford-on-Sea all close at hand. Lymington makes a good centre for exploring the New Forest, enjoying the seaside, or making trips to the Isle of Wight.

There has been a settlement at Lymington for many centuries and proximity to the New Forest ensured that in the days of wooden

ships, shipbuilding prospered there. There was also a prosperous
salt-producing industry for which Lymington was noted but the
shipbuilding declined after the coming of metal ships and
competition from the Midlands and North killed the salt trade.

Later Prosperity

The coming of the railway, and the development of the 'holiday
habit' did much to restore the fortunes and further the development
of Lymington. The ferry crossing to Yarmouth in the Isle of Wight,
the extension of the railway to serve the Pier attracted visitors and
the holiday-makers helped to make Lymington prosperous again.
It soon became much enlarged, extending to the west and south-west
and the population increased rapidly. Today it is a popular yachting
centre.

Georgian Houses

Lymington has a fine High Street where there are still some
handsome Georgian houses. At the top of High Street is the church,
St. Thomas's, with its tower crowned by a lantern-like cupola. The
windows and the piscina are worth inspecting as are the walls where
much Norman work survives.

In the churchyard lies Coventry Patmore the poet (1823–1896),
whose *Angel in the House* and other poems about love and marriage
gave a more intimate warmth to these subjects than had previously
been characteristic of Victorian poetry, where a cloying sentimentality
and complacency had hitherto ruled. Even so his efforts were very
decorous and conventional by modern standards, and much coloured
by his preoccupation with religious themes. His best, though not his
most popular works are the lesser known lyrics where his vision
extends to horizons wider than homely domestic idylls. In the
churchyard is also the town's War Memorial. The monument standing
on the higher ground is dedicated to Admiral Sir Harry Burrard-Neale
(1840).

Buckland Rings

A mile north of Lymington is Buckland Rings where, in 1744, there
was a notable find of two hundredweights of Roman coins.

Three miles to the north-west of Lymington is Sway, a large village
easily recognised form afar by its 200-feet high tower—Peterson's
Tower built 70 years ago of pure concrete. It was an effort to 'prove'
the material for building purposes.

A mile west of the town is Pennington; south and south-west along
the coast are the Salterns, where Lymington salt used to be collected.

Good Beach

Milford-on-Sea is one of the newer resorts on the coast of
Hampshire. Not only does it have a good beach, but like Lymington,
it makes an excellent centre from which to explore the New Forest.

Magnificent view towards Shaftesbury from Bulbarrow

Ashmore: peaceful and lovely Dorset village

The Rufus Stone: historic monument in New Forest

From the beach there is a fine view of ships entering and leaving the Solent, but the larger liners usually leave from Southampton, via Spithead, and the east of the Isle of Wight. The cliffs here are not very high and the Isle of Wight lies only five miles away out to sea with the Needles extending westward.

Barton on Sea

This quiet, unspoiled holiday resort is set on the low cliffs overlooking Christchurch Bay, with fine views across to the Isle of Wight and westward to Hengistbury Head. The beach is mainly sand and shingle and very popular for bathing and fishing. Inland lies New Milton with a station on the main railway line, while at Milton Green there are attractive old inns.

Hurst Castle

On a long spit of land running south-eastwards into the sea, is Hurst Castle, which dominates the entrance to the Solent. It was built as part of coastal defences by order of Henry VIII. Dating from about 1539–1540 the structure has a twelve-sided tower in the centre, surrounded by a curtain wall from which jut the three bastions. It was allowed to decay for many years but by 1635 repeated requests for restoration and new stores resulted in sufficient repair work to make the place worth occupation by Cromwellian forces. In 1648, the year before his trial, Charles I was prisoner here. Although it was planned to dismantle it after the Stuart Restoration, this was not done, and through succeeding centuries various defensive uses were found for Hurst Castle. Although in 1933 the War Office gave the property into the care of the Ministry of Works (now the Department of the Environment), they 'borrowed' it again for a garrison during World War II.

This old fortress is very interesting and well worth a visit. The public is admitted on most weekdays, and on Sundays at 2 p.m.

Bird Sanctuary

North-east of the Shingles is Keyhaven, a small and very quiet resort frequented by yachtsmen. The marshes here are a bird sanctuary. A small ferryboat plies between Keyhaven and Hurst Castle, an alternative to the $1\frac{1}{2}$ mile walk along the beach.

Hythe

Hythe is situated on the western shore of Southampton Water, facing the docks and with the New Forest stretching inland to the west. It is really, in effect, a suburb of Southampton and the large majority of its inhabitants cross by the ferry to Southampton every day to work. It is an attractive leafy little place and fine views of Southampton can be obtained from its shoreline.

Three miles south-east of Hythe, on Southampton Water, and two miles north-west of where it opens into the Solent, is Fawley.

F

Fawley is famous for its great oil refinery, built in Cadland Park, formerly the ancestral home of the Drummond family.

Calshot

This small village with a spit of land extending into Southampton Water, is situated due south of Fawley. It was once famous as a seaplane base but today it is a favourite sight-seeing spot and picnic centre. Great ships, hovercraft and hydrofoils may be seen very clearly with binoculars. There are ample parking facilities.

At the tip of the spit of land east of the village, stands Calshot Castle, built by order of Henry VIII with stones from Beaulieu Abbey.

RINGWOOD

Population: 10,000
Early Closing Days: Monday/Thursday
Market Day: Wednesday

ALTHOUGH OUTSIDE THE AREA of the New Forest, Ringwood makes a good centre for exploring the western side of it. In fact, places like Burley (four miles east), as well as the heaths and woodlands round about can be explored more easily from Ringwood and neighbouring Fordingbridge than from places on the eastern side.

The parish church is dedicated to Saints Peter and Paul and is Early English in style. Cruciform in shape it was largely rebuilt in 1854, but retains many of its ancient features, including a twelfth-century double piscina to the south-east of the chancel. There is a notable brass to John Prophete, Dean of Hereford and York, who died in 1416.

Monmouth

The Duke of Monmouth was captured after his abortive rebellion in 1685 at a farm near Horton in Dorset, some eight miles west of Ringwood, but he was brought back to the White Hart Inn at Ringwood as a prisoner. It was here that he penned his famous appeal to James II, his uncle, begging for mercy, which was refused. This inn, with other views in and around the place, has been painted by Sir David Murray, R.A. Close by the Avon here, Monmouth's house still stands; here he was kept for several more days after his initial capture. Nearby are some attractive thatched cottages.

Matcham Park

Four miles to the south-west of Ringwood is Matcham Park, a large sporting arena and stadium, still under development. Here stock-car racing, horse-riding events and other activities are held.

Tyrrell's Ford

About three miles due south of Ringwood is the traditional spot on the Avon River known as Tyrrell's Ford, it being alleged that this was where Sir Walter Tyrrell crossed when he fled after his accidental, or otherwise, killing of the king, William Rufus in 1100. But since there was a fourteenth-century Tyrrell who owned nearby Avon Tyrrell, the name may derive from him.

Two miles south from the Ford is Sopley which has a thirteenth-century church built on top of a Celtic mound, a practice found frequently in Hampshire. Sopley church has some interesting features, notably two carved stone figures, probably representing founders of the church.

Ellingham

North of Ringwood is Ellingham which has a twelfth-century Priory Church, St. Mary and All Saints, with a fine fifteenth-century screen and other interesting features.

FORDINGBRIDGE

Population: 5,100
Early Closing Day: Thursday

FORDINGBRIDGE IS ON THE RIVER AVON, six miles north of Ringwood, and is the best centre for exploring the north-western area of the New Forest. It derives its name from the fourteenth-century, seven-arched bridge, which has been several times widened and is now an ancient monument.

Domesday Mention

This place was always a settlement and is mentioned in Domesday Book under the name of 'Forde' when it already had a church and two mills. The church, St. Mary's, is a building of stone and flint and combines Early English, Early Decorated and later styles in an agreeable manner. The fine chancel roof is of oak and the south wall still has its Norman doorway. There is an interesting fifteenth-century chapel.

The churchyard contains a fine avenue of limes and sugar-loaf shaped yew trees and on the outside wall of the church there is a 'miracle stone', a sixteenth-century altar-tomb.

The great artist Augustus John spent his last years at Fordingbridge, dying there in 1961.

Museums

Breamore, which is just over three miles north of Fordingbridge, has a delightful Saxon church and a fine Elizabethan manor house, situated in beautiful parkland overlooking the Avon valley. It is noted for its fine tapestries, paintings and furniture, among many other treasures. There are two museums in the grounds: one is the Carriage Museum which houses a number of horse-drawn vehicles, the other is the Countryside Museum, depicting rural arts and crafts.

Roman Villa

Situated four miles north-west of Fordingbridge, Rockbourne is an attractive village with a fine old church, manor house and inn. To the south of the village is Rockbourne Roman Villa, discovered beneath the village cricket green. It has been revealed as an establishment of considerable size and importance with scores of rooms. The foundations which remain show the sophisticated heating system, bath and cooking areas as well as some fine mosaic tiling. At the site is the Morley Hewitt Museum with a large collection of items found during the excavations and various other antiquities.

SOUTHAMPTON

Population: 213,750
Early Closing Days: Monday and Wednesday
Market Days: Friday and Saturday
Tourist Information Centre: (N) Canute Road
                                      (L) The Precinct, Above Bar

SOUTHAMPTON IS BRITAIN'S LEADING PORT and calls itself, very proudly, the 'Gateway of England'. For countless thousands of people, especially from the United States and other countries on the American continent, Southampton is the first British city they see. This entry to Britain is indeed an impressive one with the many maritime activities in Southampton Water, the vast Fawley Oil Refinery complex to the west and the occasional glimpses of green shores on either bank, terminating at the great port set at the head of this long stretch of almost land-locked water.

Clean City

For the holiday-maker Southampton itself is of absorbing interest. There are the great ocean liners to be seen, tours to be made of the various docks, or perhaps a trip on the later forms of transport—the hovercraft and the hydrofoil. Southampton has been largely rebuilt following the heavy bombing it suffered at the hands of the German Luftwaffe during the Second World War, and it is now characterised by fine wide streets, new parades of handsome shops and an unusually large number of parks. Not only does it appear an exceptionally clean city, but in the centre of the place one is never very far from some handsome open space or green corner.

Roman City

The original settlement was made by the Romans when Clausentum grew up as the port for Venta Belgarum, or Winchester as we know it. It was not on the site of the present city centre, but more in the area of Bitterne railway station on the east bank of the River Itchen. When the Romans went, the Saxons moved the settlement to its present position between the Rivers Test and Itchen and it was they who called it Hamtun, or Hamptoune. It soon rivalled Winchester in importance and gave its name to the whole county which became known as Hamtumscyre.

In 962, during the reign of King Edgar, a charter granted to the town gives the name as Suthamptoune, and the Elizabethan poet Michael Drayton, in his great patriotic poem *Polyolbion*, devotes many alexandrines to the legendary tales of Sir Bevis of Hamptoun, and celebrates the general beauty of this part of England.

In 837 the Danes came raiding and their raids went on intermittently until Canute the Dane was elected king by the Anglo-Saxon Council in 1017. Southampton disputes with Bosham the claim that it was on the shore-line there that this extraordinarily gifted ruler demonstrated to his flattering courtiers that no mortal man, however great a king, could possibly control, let alone turn back, the relentlessly incoming sea. A notice above an inn doorway in Canute Road makes this claim very boldly, stating that it was upon that very spot, which was then the beach, that this favourite historic tale was born.

After the Conquest

After the Norman Conquest the importance of Southampton increased rapidly for it was the main port for Normandy and the new ruler of Britain and his followers went back and forth regularly between the two countries.

In 1189, the army of the Third Crusade left from Southampton and it is on record that the town supplied 800 hogs to the fleet victuallers. Charters were granted by Henry I and Henry II, while King John granted the town two fresh charters, the second of which was confirmed by his son, Henry III in 1227.

The port was busy throughout the dispute with France known to history as the Hundred Years War. The French attacked the town in 1338, but seven years later Edward III and the Black Prince sailed for the renewed campaigns which gave the English the resounding victory of Crécy. From here too, sailed the forces of Henry V, as Shakespeare reminds us with the words spoken by Chorus:

'The well-appointed king at Hampton pier
Embarks his royalty. . . .'

Later lines describe the bustle of the port, the ship-boys climbing the rigging, and the whistles sounding as 'sails this fleet majestical'.

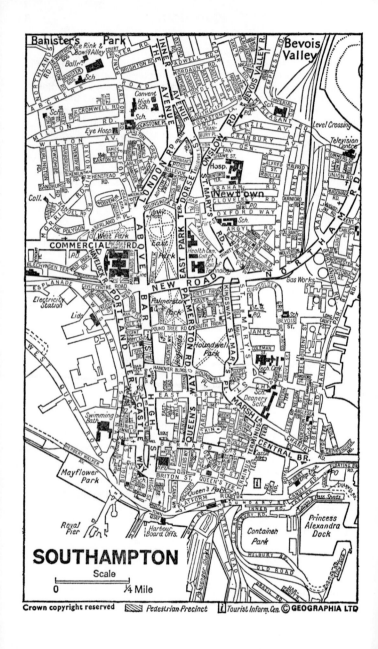

SOUTHAMPTON

Scale

0   ¼ Mile

Crown copyright reserved   ▨ Pedestrian Precinct   ⓘ Tourist Inform. Cen. ©️ GEOGRAPHIA LTD

It was typical of the times, of course, that this lively departure scene was preceded by the execution of the Earl of Cambridge, Sir Thomas Grey and Lord Scrope before the Bargate at Southampton. Henry had discovered their plots against him and dealt with the matter with characteristic firmness and promptitude.

Pilgrim Fathers

In 1620, this flourishing port saw the fitting out and provisioning of two ships whose names have echoed through world history ever since. These were the vessels *Mayflower* and *Speedwell* in which the refugees whom we now call the Pilgrim Fathers, sailed for the New World in search of religious freedom.

During the Civil War in England Southampton was a notable Parliamentary centre and was for a time blockaded by the Royalist forces. But following the Civil War the activity of the port declined because of the rise of the rival ports of Poole and Portsmouth.

A new life came to the place with the discovery in the eighteenth century of mineral springs so that Southampton became known as a spa. Visitors flocked to the seaside to enjoy the air and 'take the waters' and the long sea-shore soon made the place popular. There was also a revival of ship-building activity on the Itchen side and the town became very busy during the Napoleonic Wars and prospered accordingly.

Railway Development

In 1838 new docks were built and the coming of the railway two years later contributed to the steady growth and rising importance of Southampton. At first the town developed close to the artificial tongue of land jutting out from the southern end of the peninsula but as the development progressed the suburbs spread out far beyond the limits of the dock area. During the First World War thousands of troops poured through the Southampton docks en route to the various theatres of war. In 1927 the Southern Railway began work on reclaiming the expanse of muddy land on the north side of the Test estuary from Southampton's western shore to Millbrook point and by 1934 the new Western Docks had been completed on the outer edge of the reclaimed land. Southampton then suffered the worst ordeal in its long history during the Second World War when it became a prime target for enemy bombers. Not only did troops embark and disembark there but its commercial activities were of prime importance too. At the time of Dunkerque a vast number of men were repatriated through the port.

Reconstruction

In the post-war years Southampton grew busy again, and the work of reconstruction went ahead. By 1964, when the sovereign granted Southampton a charter making it a city, there was already a fine new town centre and the former University College, incorporated fifty years earlier, became the University of Southampton.

Always keenly interested in progress, the city saw the first regular hovercraft service in the country plying between Southampton and Cowes, Isle of Wight, opened in 1966. In July 1967 the railway was electrified and the journey between the port and London now takes only just over the hour.

The present city centre is an interesting mixture of the old and the new and a pleasant place to linger. The main thoroughfare is High Street and its continuation, Above Bar, north of the Bargate which marks the boundary of the medieval town.

New Road runs eastward from the Clock Tower in Above Bar and is the main eastern artery. A little further to the north Commercial Road runs westward and is, in fact, the beginning of the main route to the west. The corner of Above Bar and Commercial Road is known as the Junction, and from here it is easy to make a tour of the historic buildings of the city centre.

Spitfire Museum

South of Commercial Road, and turning west out of Havelock Road, is Kingsbridge Lane with the R. J. Mitchell Memorial Hall. This is a Museum dedicated to the memory of the designer of the famous Spitfire 1 fighter plane which was so instrumental in giving the R.A.F. victory in the Battle of Britain in 1940.

Mitchell was an aircraft designer with Vickers Aircraft but before he died in 1937 he knew that his latest design had made a successful test run and would do all that was asked of it. The Museum houses a Spitfire as well as the S6B Schneider Trophy Seaplane (also Mitchell's work and from which his battle-winning plane derived).

There are many of Mitchell's papers on show, along with models, plans, drawings and photographs.

The A.T.C. cadets look after the Museum, and it was they who got the exhibits ready for showing to the public.

Link With Titanic

In Commercial Road is West Park with a memorial to Dr. Isaac Watts, the hymn-writer and another to those killed in the First World War. Across Above Bar from West Park lies East Park which contains a memorial to the *Titanic* passengers and crew lost when this famous vessel sank on her maiden voyage after hitting an iceberg on April 15th, 1912. South of Commerical Road is the striking white building of the Civic Centre dominated by its slender Clock Tower. The foundation stone was laid in 1930 by the Duke of York, later George VI. The completed buildings were opened officially by the Duke and Duchess of Gloucester in April 1939. This building is in four main sections; the Central Public Library and Art Gallery facing north, the Law Courts and Police Offices facing west—this is the block with the Clock Tower rising from it—

the Municipal Offices facing south on to Civic Centre Road and the Guildhall facing east. Here meetings and social functions take place and plays are performed. In the Civic Centre is housed the City Regalia, the archives and various treasures including a grant to the Earl of Warwick bearing the signature of the Black Prince. A charming garden belonging to the Centre has roses and unusual trees in it.

Bargate

The Civic Centre was built on a site called West Marlands which is derived from Magdalens. It once belonged to the Hospital of St. Mary Magdalene, devoted to lepers who were not allowed inside the town walls. The route down Above Bar from the Junction passes a Clock Tower built in 1889, standing where New Road branches eastward. Houndwell Park lies southwards and leads on to Bargate. This was the north gate and principal entrance to the old town. Here the civic dignitaries welcomed important visitors and here too were exhibited the heads of the Earl of Cambridge, with Grey and Scrope after their execution by order of Henry V. On the south side is a statue of George III in Roman costume. Inside Bargate is the old Guildhall, converted into a museum after the new Guildhall at the Civic Centre came into being.

Until 1937 all traffic had to pass through Bargate—including the old trams—but after that the houses on the east side were demolished and space was made to carry the southbound traffic. These new buildings survived the air-raids already mentioned, but those on the west did not, so in 1945 a way was made round the west side also and the Bargate became an island, closed to traffic.

Ancient Towers

Westwards, on the corner of Bargate Street and Western Shore Road is the thirteenth-century Arundel, or Windwhistle Tower, marking the turn in the walls which from here ran southward, following the Western Shore Road. The walls, with arcading, are in an almost perfect state of preservation here. The other towers are Catchcold Tower (fifteenth-century), and Garderobe Tower (fifteenth-century). At the corner of Simnel Street is Biddlesgate. The Forty Steps lead up to Albion Place on Lansdowne Hill. South of Simnel Street are the Postern Gate and the fourteenth-century West Gate, the latter being in an excellent state of preservation. The West Quay was at one time situated in front.

Pilgrim Fathers' Memorial

Beyond the West Gate is the Pilgrim Fathers' Memorial, commemorating the departure of the Pilgrim Fathers who sailed for America from this spot. A further plaque commemorates the U.S. Forces who sailed from there to begin the Second Front landings in 1944. Nearby is the Stella Fountain dedicated to the

Stewardess Mary Ann Rogers who was drowned while helping passengers when the *Stella* went down in 1899. Opposite are the West Docks and the famous Skyway Hotel. Three stone cannon balls dating from the time of King Henry V are here built into the walls.

Tudor House

Western Shore Road here becomes Town Quay. In Bugle Street is the fourteenth-century Wool House which contains a Maritime Museum. The street leads on to St. Michael's Square with the magnificent old Tudor House standing on the west side. The basement of this edifice dates from a considerably earlier period; inside the house is a most interesting museum. Opposite is St. Michael's, the oldest of the city churches (it dates from the eleventh century), reconstructed in 1828 and saved from destruction in 1940 by the personal bravery of one of the churchwardens. The high spire was built in 1732 and served as a landmark. North of St. Michael's Square is the site of Southampton Castle.

Merchant Navy Memorial

In High Street stand the ruins of Holyrood Church, built in 1320 and destroyed in 1940, but preserved as a Memorial to the men of the Merchant Navy. To the north and on the same side of High Street stand the Dolphin and Star Hotels. The Dolphin has been on its present site for four centuries and the Star Hotel is almost as old. Down High Street, just before the Town Quay is reached, is Winkle Street where there is God's House (Maison Dieu), once a twelfth-century Hospice, or shelter for poor travellers. Its endowments were used by Edward III in 1340 when he founded Queen's College, Oxford, to which control of the Hospice passed. Nearby is the old Bowling Green, dating from 1299.

Docks and Railways

Southampton Docks were begun in 1838, and the Outer Dock was completed in 1842. The docks were built on an artificial peninsula jutting southwards into Southampton Water from the southern end of the natural peninsula on which Southampton stands. They were owned by the Southampton Dock Company until 1892 when they were acquired by the London and South Western Railway They passed to the Southern Railway in 1923 and in 1948 were nationalised and transferred to the British Transport Commission, who in turn, passed them to the British Transport Docks Board, the present owners. They are administered by the Southampton Harbour Board.

The artificial peninsula contains all the old docks. The docks are walled off from the city and only passengers or those meeting or seeing them off are allowed in the dock area. Exception is made for the conducted tours. On the left-hand pillar of No 2 Gate is a bronze plaque commemorating the Old Contemptibles who embarked from Southampton Dock in 1914.

Continental Ferries

The Outer Dock, the east side which opens on to the Itchen, was one of the original docks and is now used by the various drive-on, drive-off ferries to various Continental ports. The adjacent Inner Dock was recently filled in to provide a site for a passenger reception hall, approach road, container parks and vehicle check-points. South of the Outer Dock is Empress Dock, opened by Queen Victoria in 1890. Jutting southward from Empress Dock is the Prince of Wales Dry Dock, opened by the then Prince of Wales (later Edward VII), in 1895. It is 745 feet long by 91 feet wide and can be used for ships of up to 25,000 tons. At the most southerly point of the peninsula is the Queen Elizabeth II Terminal for passengers and cargo, opened in 1966 by Queen Elizabeth II. From this point too, all ships are signalled in or out of the docks.

Ocean Terminal

On the western side of the docks the most important feature is Ocean Dock, opened in 1911, which is the centre for the North Atlantic passenger trade. In this dock is moored a 150-ton floating crane. Ocean Terminal, opened in 1950, runs alongside the eastern part of Ocean Dock. Boat trains start from and terminate here and on top there is a Sightseers' Balcony. The Terminal is almost a quarter of a mile long and one of the finest in the world. West of Ocean Dock is Trafalgar Day Dock, opened on 21st October, (Trafalgar Day), 1905. It is 912 feet long by 100 feet wide, and most ships using the docks can be accommodated.

Royal Pier

Between the Old and New Docks are the Town Quay and the Royal Pier, both under the jurisdiction of the Harbour Board. The Town Quay is the oldest piece of dockland in Southampton. The first pier on this site was built in 1411 and its successor was taken over by the old Pier and Harbour Commission in 1803. It is used for the ferry to Hythe and for coastal and Isle of Wight trade. The Royal Pier was opened in 1833 by the Princess (later Queen) Victoria and is used for ferries to the Isle of Wight. Launches taking visitors on tours of the Docks also start from the Royal Pier.

New Docks

West of the Royal Pier are the New, or Western Docks, built between 1927 and 1934 by the Southern Railway. To do this the mud of the bay west of Southampton had to be reclaimed. Originally five jetties projecting into the River Test were planned, but these ideas were later abandoned in favour of a straight quay, $1\frac{1}{2}$ miles long and dredged deep enough to take the world's largest liners. To the west is the George V Dry Dock, opened by George V in 1933 and one of the largest dry docks in the world. It is 1,200 feet long, 135 feet wide and 59 feet deep. It can accommodate vessels of up to 100,000 tons.

Expansion
Like most towns and cities, Southampton has grown considerably in size in recent years and now extends for over a mile in all landward directions from its original nucleus, the old medieval town. Beyond the first suburbs there sprawl now many more, standing where once was open country.

To the north the London Road becomes the Avenue leading to the Common, an area of heathland some 375 acres in extent. This is a survival of the huge forests which once characterised this part of South Hampshire. Of the pools to be found there, one is for paddling and one is for bathing. In the southern part may be found the cemetery, also the Southampton Zoo. Between this Common and Polygon (once the fashionable centre of the city), is the County Cricket Ground.

EASTLEIGH

Population: 47,000
Early Closing Day: Wednesday
Market Day: Thursday

EASTLEIGH IS AN INDUSTRIAL TOWN five miles to the north of Southampton and like most places in Hampshire, it is remarkably clean. It developed in the mid-nineteenth century as a railway junction and the main contruction and repair works of the old London and South-Western Railway.

It is built on on a gridiron pattern with most of the streets set at right-angles to one another. The railway works are on the east side, near the River Itchen, on the west side of which the town stands. Across the Itchen is Bishopstoke which is much older than Eastleigh and gave its name to the railway station for the first few years of its existence.

South of Eastleigh is the Southampton Airport, built originally for the American Naval Air Services during the First World War. It was much enlarged in the years following the Second World War and is 374 acres in extent. Services link Southampton with the Channel Islands and France.

Ghostly Ruin
South-east from Southampton and barely beyond its border lies Netley Abbey, a magnificent Cistercian edifice built by monks from

Beaulieu when they settled on this eastern shore of Southampton Water. Richard Barham (Tom Ingoldsby), wrote verses about this romantic ruin in the nineteenth century and it has much the same aspect now as it had then:

'I saw thee Netley, as the sun
Across the western wave,
Was sinking low, and a golden glow
To thy roofless towers he gave.'

But Barham's poem goes on to describe how that benign looking place had been the scene of terrible inhumanity such as the walling up alive of an errant nun. There are many legends and ghost stories attached to this forlorn pile, shaded by trees and shrubs, and at least one concerns a man who died of fright after examining an underground passage there.

The original Abbey Gatehouse was converted to a fort by Henry VIII, and became the site of Netley Castle which is still in use today and is administered by the Department of the Environment.

Yachting Centres

Some two miles south-east from Netley, where the Hamble River joins Southampton Water, is Hamble, a yachting centre of some renown. Here there are steep, winding streets lined with old cottages and inns, leading down towards the river bank. St. Andrew's Church, rebuilt by William of Wykeham, has much Norman detail. Across the river from Hamble is Warsash, another yachting centre. These two places already have a niche in history as the landing points of the marauding Saxons, Danes and French and others who have attempted to assault these shores.

Patron of Shakespeare

About seven miles south-east from Southampton is Titchfield, an historic town with numerous seventeenth- and eighteenth-century buildings. The old church is full of interest for much thirteenth- and fourteenth-century work survives including the sedilia, piscina and the Priest's Doorway. In the Abbot's Chapel is the striking marble and alabaster tomb of two Earls of Southampton, with dramatic carvings, shields and heraldic beasts. One of these Earls was the grandfather of Shakespeare's patron, Henry Wriothsley, the third Earl.

North of the town is the ruined Titchfield Abbey, built originally by Premonstratensian monks, converted after the Dissolution into a private residence and renamed Place House. It is now administered by the Department of the Environment.

William Cobbett

Along the banks of the River Hamble, some five miles out of Southampton, is Botley, a notable strawberry-growing centre and a

market gardening locality. Here lived William Cobbett, the author of
Rural Rides, who was a Radical M.P. There is a modern memorial
commemorating his association with the town. There is really
charming riverside scenery here and the National Trust control a
large portion of it.

PORTSMOUTH

Population: 207,040
Early Closing Days: Monday/Wednesday
Tourist Information Centres: (N) Albert Johnson Dock
                                  (R) Clarence Parade
                                  (L) Guildhall

FAMOUS SEAPORT, IMPORTANT COMMERCIAL CENTRE and
also a holiday resort, Portsmouth (with Southsea) is a thriving modern
community with many fascinating aspects, not the least of which is
the world-renowned Royal Naval Dockyard. Situated on an island of
considerable size with immense, almost land-locked harbours to east
and west, it was inevitable that Portsmouth should become
identified with seafaring activities. Although a small community
existed along by Portsmouth Harbour from the eleventh century, it
was not until the reign of Henry VIII that Portsmouth sprang into
prominence with the establishment of a Dockyard for the Royal
Navy.
    The 'early' city was heavily fortified and became one of the
important defence points of the south coast of England,
continuing to grow in importance during Britain's great naval
build-up. It was to become, centuries later, one of the most
important of world naval ports. The fortifications which can be seen
still, are of eighteenth-century origin but the Tudor defences may also
be detected in places, in the area known as 'Old Town'.
    Modern Portsmouth with fashionable Southsea as its holiday wing
has spread far and wide beyond the small fortified 'Old Town' from
which it developed, extending beyond its one-time island
boundaries to take in a large area of the mainland.
    Today, with development proceeding apace, a vast community
lies between the waters of Portsmouth and Langstone Harbours,
linked by bridge and modern roads, to the mainland, by ferry to
Gosport across the mouth of Portsmouth Harbour and by ferries and
hovercraft to the Isle of Wight. For passengers only there is a ferry
across the mouth of Langstone Harbour to Hayling Island.

Royal Dockyard
    The main gateway to the Royal Dockyard is in The Hard, in the
district of Portsea, and within the three hundred acres which it

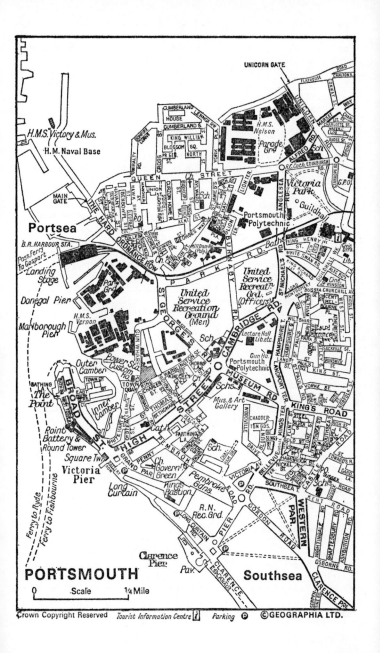

PORTSMOUTH

Southsea

UNICORN GATE

H.M.S.Victory & Mus.
H.M. Naval Base

Portsea

MAIN
GATE

B.R. HARBOUR STA.
Pass. Ferry
To Gosport
Landing
Stage

Donegal Pier

Marlborough
Pier

H.M.S.
Vernon

Outer
Camber

The Point
BATHING

Point
Battery &
Round Tower
Square Twr

Victoria
Pier

Ferry to Ryde
Ferry to Fishbourne

Long
Curtain

Clarence
Pier

Pav.

CUMBERLAND
HOUSE
CUMBERLAND S.
KING WILLIAM
BLOSSOM SQ.
PR. GEO.
ST.
NORTH

H.M.S.
Nelson

Parade
Grd.

ALFRED RD.
Sch.

R.C. Cath. EDINBURGH
RD.

Victoria
Park

Guildhall

QUEEN STREET

Portsmouth
Polytechnic

PARK RD. Baths

KING HENRY ST.

WHITE SWAN RD.
Lib.

United
Service
Recreatn.
Grd.
(Officers)

United
Service
Recreation
Ground
(Men)

Sch.

Lecture Hall
Lib. etc.

Gun Ho.
Portsmouth
Polytechnic

CAMBRIDGE RD.

KING'S ROAD

MUSEUM RD.

LANDPORT TER.

Sch.

Mus. & Art
Gallery

Town Quay

Inner
Camber

Cath.

Farthing
LA.

Sch.

Govern
Green
Ch.

Pembroke
Gdns.

Kings
Bastion

R.N.
Rec. Grd.

LONG CURTAIN

VICTORIA RD.

GORDON ROAD

WESTERN PAR.

PIER

CLARENCE ESPLANADE

CLARENCE PDE.

0   Scale   ¼ Mile

Crown Copyright Reserved   Tourist Information Centre ⓘ   Parking Ⓟ   ©GEOGRAPHIA LTD.

covers are docks, dry-docks, slipways and wharves, workshop stores, fitting-out basins, factories, etc., together with some fine eighteenth-century buildings. Ahead from the main gateway is H.M.S. *Victory*, the flagship of Admiral Lord Nelson, and veteran ship of the battles at Cape St. Vincent, Gibraltar, Toulon and Trafalgar, and today the Flagship of the Commander-in-Chief, Portsmouth.

Nearby is the Victory Museum, with a fine collection of naval relics, the emphasis being on things connected with Nelson. A panorama of the Battle of Trafalgar brings that famous naval triumph to life so that modern visitors may have the scene clear in their minds and appreciate the tactics which made and kept Britain 'Mistress of the Seas'. Both *Victory* and the Museum are open daily.

Garrison Church

Situated off Pembroke Road is the Garrison Church, an interesting old building which originated as the Hospital of St. Nicholas. It became the Governor's House and was the scene of the marriage of Charles II with Catherine of Braganza. More recently the building, which dated from the thirteenth century, was much damaged by enemy action during the Second World War. General Napier, the conqueror of Sind, who sent the famous code report 'Peccavi' (meaning ostensibly 'I have sinned' but conveying news of his brilliant campaign in this district which is now part of West Pakistan), lies buried in the churchyard, his tomb being opposite the west door. In neighbouring Pembroke Gardens there is a fine statue of Lord Nelson.

Cathedrals

The Cathedral Church of St. Thomas of Canterbury was, originally, the parish church. Founded in the twelfth century it has been much rebuilt, especially in the seventeenth century. The tower dates from this period. Much additional building began after the church was raised to Cathedral status in 1927. In the interior there is a notable twelfth-century chancel and transepts.

The Cathedral of St. John, in the Edinburgh Road, is a nineteenth-century edifice of some attractiveness. There is a particularly handsome Lady Chapel. It is in a nice setting, opposite Victoria Park where there is beautiful rose garden, fine monuments and a charming Aviary.

Buckingham House

In the old High Street there were once many fine period houses but owing to devastation during the Second World War only Buckingham House survives. A plaque affixed to the wall records that it was here, in 1628, that George Villiers, first Duke of Buckingham, was assassinated by John Felton, a fanatical (and somewhat deranged) soldier, as the Duke was about to depart to the relief of the besieged French Protestants at La Rochelle.

Some of the famous New Forest ponies

Palace House Beaulieu, the Montagu Mansion

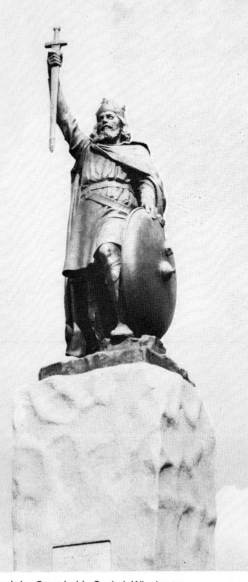

Statue of Alfred the Great in his Capital, Winchester

The Guildhall

In Guildhall Square, near Portsmouth and Southsea Station is the Guildhall, opened by the Prince of Wales (afterwards Edward VII) in 1890. It is a most attractive edifice with a tall, ornamental clock-tower and handsome columns flanked by sculptured lions. Apart from housing the Civic offices of the City Council, Guildhall contains historic maces, bowls, flagons and plate.

Charles Dickens

Northwards from the Station, along the Commercial Road is the house where Charles Dickens was born in 1812. It is built in red brick, with two storeys and an attic. The wall bears a plaque inscribed: 'Charles Dickens, Birthplace, February 7th, 1812.' Now a museum the house is furnished in period style and contains many Dickensian relics, engravings, books, furniture, etc. It is open daily to the public.

City Museum and Art Gallery

In Alexandra Road, off the High Street, is the City Museum and Art Gallery with a collection showing local archaeology and history, furniture and glassware, pottery and prints, paintings etc. It is open to the public from March to October.

At the end of High Street, where it joins Broad Street, is the Square Tower, part of the King's Bastion fortifications. On one wall of the Tower there is a bust of Charles I with details of his journeys to France and Spain. Close by is the Sally Port giving access to the Harbour where, in earlier days the boats carried sailors out to their ships at Spithead when they returned from shore leave.

Royal Marines Museum

Housed in the former Officers' Mess of Eastney Barracks, in the Cromwell Road, the Museum shows a chronological history of the Royal Marines from 1664 onwards.

There are fine collections of uniforms, badges, medals etc., including the ten V.C.s won by Marines. Cars are parked on the vast Old Parade Ground, and admission is free. The Museum is open all the year except Christmas and Boxing Days.

In nearby Henderson Road is the Eastney Pumping Station with its reciprocal steam pumps by Boulton and Watt, installed in 1887: adjacent is a Crossley Gas Engine from 1904. Both can be seen at weekends from April to September.

SOUTHSEA

As the residential and holiday suburb of Portsmouth, Southsea may rightly claim to be a seaside resort of handsome proportions. Its wide, tree-lined roads lead down to a most attractive sea-front backed by Southsea Common, a splendid open space adorned with

G

water gardens, rock gardens and formal gardens. There are good sports facilities, such as tennis courts, putting greens, paddling and swimming pools, and also a Children's Corner.

The broad Esplanade is a long one, extending from Clarence Pier, where the Hovercraft service to Ryde leaves, eastwards to South Parade Pier and well beyond it. Along the Esplanade are several interesting monuments, not the least of which is the great anchor belonging to *Victory*, mounted high for all to see its massive proportions. On the Esplanade too there is a huge Naval War Memorial and the Castle constructed originally by order of Henry VIII —considerably rebuilt in the nineteenth century. Along the Eastern Parade is the Cumberland House Museum and Art Gallery, open daily to the public. From the sand and shingle beach there is excellent bathing, and fine views out over Spithead to the Isle of Wight.

GOSPORT

Gosport may be reached via the floating bridge, by steamer across Portsmouth Harbour, or by road via the Fareham route to the north. It is an important seaport, naval station and yachting centre, situated to the west of Portsmouth Harbour, overlooking Spithead and the Solent towards the Isle of Wight.

At Holy Trinity Church in The Hard (dating from the seventeenth century but largely rebuilt), is an organ which came from the former mansion of the Duke of Chandos in Edgware. It is thought to have been played by Handel who was for a time in residence at *Canons*, the Duke's home.

The huge Royal Naval Hospital in the Haslar area overlooks Spithead. It dates from the eighteenth century, while on the sea wall stands Fort Blockhouse, defending the entrance to Portsmouth Harbour. South of the town lies Stokes Bay, the seaside suburb with a shingle beach, but excellent bathing and sports facilities.

LEE-ON-SOLENT

This is an unspoiled seaside resort with a long, open expanse along the sea shore and a splendid entertainments Pavilion. Just to the north of the town there is an important airfield. The shingle beach affords good bathing although there is a heated open-air swimming pool for those who prefer it. Westwards lies Hill Head, a residential locality at the mouth of Titchfield Haven where yachting and boating is the popular pastime.

FAREHAM

North-west from Gosport is the fast-growing town of Fareham, with a long and very busy main street. It is situated on a tidal creek of Portsmouth Harbour. The Church of SS. Peter and Paul, largely rebuilt, includes the chancel of the eighteenth-century edifice and on the walls there are paintings of some antiquity. William Makepeace Thackeray lived in Fareham as a boy. About two miles to the north-west is Boarhunt, with an old church of Saxon origin from which the chancel arch, font and a window survive.

Portsdown Hill

This is the lofty hill ridge on the landward side of Portsmouth, where Lord Palmerston built a chain of forts during the Napoleonic Wars. There is also a Nelson Monument, 120 feet high, with the details of the Battle of Trafalgar (1805), inscribed upon the base. A good road provides access to the whole length of the hill, affording magnificent panoramic views over Portsmouth, its harbours, and across the sea to the Isle of Wight beyond.

Roman Legacy

Situated north-west of Portsmouth, below Portsdown Hill and on the north shore of Portsmouth Harbour, Portchester is a fast growing village. The substantial ruin of Portchester Castle is a legacy from the Romans for it was they who built the massive stone walls which surround the site, directly overlooking the harbour.

Later a Norman castle and a Priory were built within the walls and in the fourteenth century the place became a palace. The castle ruins are a massive reminder of the skills of our ancestors, while the little Church of St. Mary, derived from the Priory, is a gem of its kind, and has a lovely west front. Inside there is a Norman font and the Royal Arms of Elizabeth I and Queen Anne. It is open to the public on weekdays, and on Sunday mornings during summer.

SOUTHWICK

On the other side of Portsdown Hill, to the north, lies Southwick, a rural locality with charming houses and a restored twelfth-century church of much interest. In the interior are altar candlesticks from a vanished twelfth-century Priory, and some notable woodwork. The tomb of John White and his family is interesting.

College Founder

Wickham is an attractive village, situated to the north-west of Southwick with some fine old Georgian buildings and a broad Market Square. Here Bishop William of Wykeham was born in 1324. This distinguished churchman, Bishop of Winchester and at one time Lord Chancellor to Edward III, is remembered today as the founder of Winchester College (which has for a motto his favourite maxim: 'Manners makyth Man'), also of New College, Oxford. The Chesapeake Flour Mill in Wickham is believed to have been constructed from the timbers of the famous captive American warship, seized by Britain during the War of Independence.

Aylward Cross

Just north-east of Portsmouth is the old market town of Havant where the waters of Langstone Harbour provide yachting and fishing facilities. The Church, parts of which are Norman, including a window in the transept, has a most unusual chancel roof of chalk. The Aylward Cross in the chancel dates from the fifteenth century. Near the church there is a delightful old inn and a number of charming old houses.

Warblington Castle

Just east of Havant lies Warblington with a very ancient church showing traces of Saxon, Norman and later building. The doorways to the tower are Saxon and so is the mass dial on the wall, while the timbered porch is fifteenth-century. In the churchyard, note the elaborately inscribed eighteenth-century tombs, and two interesting 'watchers huts', built for guards against the body-snatchers whose activities were rife in the nineteenth century. An ancient yew tree still stands sentinel there, and not far away is all that remains of Warblington Castle.

Some two miles eastwards out of Havant is Emsworth, a tiny port on Chichester Harbour, busy with boat-building and saw-milling. It affords good facilities for boating, fishing and yachting.

HAYLING ISLAND

Due south of Havant and over a modern bridge is Hayling Island, a seaside holiday centre with various holiday camps and caravan sites. The splendid sands afford good bathing facilities along the southern shore. East and west respectively are the wide waterways of Chichester Harbour and Langstone Harbour and from Sinah Point in the south-west corner a passenger ferry runs to Eastney. In South Hayling is the Early English St. Mary's Church which has a Norman font, and in the churchyard is one of Hampshire's oldest yew trees. Near it stand the old stocks. St. Peter's church in North Hayling has three very old bells dating from the fourteenth century and still set in their original frames. There is some fine woodwork to be seen.

HAMBLEDON

Due north from Portsmouth on the London Road, Waterlooville is quickly reached. This is an expanding main road development which is almost an extension of Havant, being set where the A3 crosses the B2150 road. A little over four miles to the north-west is Hambledon, with Broadhalfpenny Down just under two miles north-east. This was the birthplace, in the mid-eighteenth century, of Hambledon Cricket Club, and a stone monument, set opposite the 'Bat and Ball' Inn commemorates that this was the green where these first matches were played.

Section 6 Winchester and Central Wessex

Covian

WINCHESTER

Population: 31,750
Early Closing Day: Thursday
Market Days: Monday, Wednesday and Saturday
Tourist Information Centre: (L) City Offices, Colebrook Street

WINCHESTER IS A FINE OLD CATHEDRAL CITY and the capital of England in Saxon days. It is an important centre in three main spheres, ecclesiastical, scholastic and military. There is a fine cathedral, a famous public school, and an important barracks.

Outside these spheres Winchester is a flourishing market town and an important tourist resort, visitors being attracted mainly by the cathedral, the old buildings, and the ideal location of the city as a centre for visiting Southampton, the New Forest, Salisbury, the Hampshire Downs and Portsmouth.

The area now covered by Winchester was settled about 1800 B.C., but the first inhabitants preferred hill-top sites and the first town of any size was on St. Catherine's Hill on the south-west of the present city: its ramparts can be seen to this day.

When the Belgae invaded Britain they destroyed the hill-top fortress and built the first town on the present site in the valley of the Itchen

at a point where there was a convenient patch of gravel on which
to build, and where the valley narrowed because of St. Giles' Hill
on the east. This occurred in 50 B.C. and when the Roman
occupation took place a century later, the town, known to the
Romans as Venta Belgarum, became the centre of the district with its
port at Clausentum, the forerunner of Southampton.

After the departure of the Romans at the end of the fourth century
the history of Venta Belgarum is obscure, but under the Saxons it
increased in importance and eventually became the capital of
Wessex. The place was mentioned by the Venerable Bede as 'Venta,
called by the Saxons Uintancaestir' when he recorded the founding
of a bishop's see in 674. The name Winchester eventually replaced
'Uintancaestir'.

Alfred The Great

In A.D. 829 Egbert, King of the West Saxons, united, by conquest,
the English kingdoms, and Winchester became the capital of all
England, and remained so for 250 years.

Alfred the Great was the most important king who reigned from
Winchester. He first defeated the Danes, who had sacked Winchester
as well as many other towns in England: then he rebuilt Winchester
and developed it as a centre of trade (especially wool), and learning.
After Alfred's time Winchester formed a school of calligraphy, which
became the leading such place in Europe. Canute, when he became
king in 1017, did much to beautify Winchester and increase its
prosperity: he was buried in the cathedral.

The Conqueror

Although Winchester was the capital city when William I came to
the throne in 1066, its rival, London, was increasing in importance, and
it was at Westminster that he was crowned; by the time Henry I
came to the throne in 1100, London was generally recognised as
the capital.

In 1141 Winchester suffered badly during the civil war between
Stephen and Matilda, but recovered, and continued a flourishing
centre of the wool trade.

Edward I held his first Parliament in the Great Hall of the castle
in 1272, but this was the last occasion that Winchester was treated
as the capital.

During the reign of Edward II the wool staple at Winchester was
transferred to Calais, and this heralded a period of decline. Despite
this, the city remained an important ecclesiastical and educational
centre. The public school was founded by William of Wykeham who
was bishop from 1366 to 1404.

Civil War

Henry VIII entertained Charles V, the Holy Roman Emperor, at
Winchester in 1522, and Mary I was married to Philip of Spain in

Winchester Cathedral on 25th July 1554. However, the city entered another period of decline when the Dissolution of the Monasteries caused many religious houses to close down.

Elizabeth I granted the city a charter in 1587: in the Civil War Winchester supported Charles I, but was captured by the Parliamentarians after a battle outside its walls on 12 December 1642, and recaptured by the Royalists in November 1643.

After the Roundhead victory at Cheriton in March 1644 the city of Winchester surrendered, but the castle remained loyal to the king and was not captured until October of the following year.

Expansion

In the Georgian era much rebuilding was carried out. Jane Austen died in Winchester, and John Keats spent some time here because of the beneficial climate. In the early nineteenth century Winchester began to expand once more, helped by the coming of the railway in 1840. In 1967, an electric train service from London put Winchester only a few minutes over the hour from its old rival.

Old and New

Winchester's main street is High Street which runs at right angles to the River Itchen. It begins at the West Gate to the north of which stand the County Buildings. In front is an obelisk commemorating the Great Plague of 1666. It was erected in 1759 and rebuilt in 1821. The Westgate itself contains a museum in which the exhibits include the City Chest and a collection of weights and measures dating from the time of Henry III. A fine view can be enjoyed from the battlements of the West Gate.

Castle Hill leads to the Great Hall, all that is left of the castle built by William I. Inside, on the wall, hangs the Round Table giving the name of each knight, said to have been used by King Arthur and his knights. But exhaustive tests made in 1976 show that in fact it dates from the reign of Edward III. This king was a great 'Arthurian' and wished to inspire his own soldiers with the spirit of chivalry. Sir Walter Raleigh was tried here, as was Dame Alicia Lisle, a 'victim' of Judge Jeffreys. This imposing hall is still used as a court.

Royal Statue

The City Cross is in the centre of the High Street and, at the bottom or eastern end, there is a statue of King Alfred, holding his sword aloft. This statue was erected in 1901 to celebrate the millenary of his death.

Nearby are the Guildhall and the residence of the Mayor, known as Abbey House, which is surrounded by the Abbey Gardens. St. John's Hospital, close to the King Alfred statue is of two periods: the portion to the north of High Street dates back to Saxon times, but that to the south is Victorian.

The Cathedral

The Cathedral is best approached from Little Minster Street. The City Museum which concentrates mostly on archaeological items can be seen on entering the precincts.

Winchester Cathedral, dedicated to the Holy Trinity, was begun in 1079 by Bishop Walkelyn, close to the Saxon cathedral. In the fourteenth century, reconstruction started by William of Wykeham was completed in the next one hundred years.

The Cathedral, 556 feet in length, covers a larger area than any other in Europe. All four styles, Norman, Early English, Decorated and Perpendicular are to be seen in the building.

The main entrance is by the west door, and the visitor sees the fine nave stretching out in front of him. The twelfth-century font is of black Tournai marble, and above it is the Perpendicular west window which is filled with pieces of glass smashed by the Parliamentarian soldiers.

On the south side of the Cathedral are the Chantry Chapels of William of Wykeham and Bishop Erdington. The latter was the first prelate of the Order of the Garter, and took part in the restoration of the cathedral.

The south transept contains a memorial to Samuel Wilberforce, Bishop of Salisbury, and a fine wrought iron gate, the earliest example of such work in England.

Crown copyright reserved   //////// Pedestrian Precinct   i Tourist Information Cent.   © GEOGRAPHIA LTD.

In the Chapel of Prior Sylkstede, which is now the vestry of Lay Clerks is the tomb of Izaak Walton and a window to his memory.

The north transept contains the tombs of Prebendary Iremonger and Sir Redvers Buller, a leader in the South African War.

The Chapel of the Holy Sepulchre, under the organ and adjoining the choir has some fine thirteenth-century frescoes.

The entrance to the low-vaulted crypt which preserved the plan of the original Norman church is in the south-east corner of the north transept.

A King's Tomb

The choir has two styles, Norman under the tower and Decorated in the east. In the centre is the tomb of William Rufus: the retro-choir still farther to the east is in Early English style. There is a fine wooden reredos (behind the altar) and a nineteenth-century screen separating the choir from the nave. South of the reredos is the Chantry Chapel of Bishop Fox and nearby are those of Cardinal Beaufort, and Bishop Waynflete founder of Magdalen College Oxford, as well as the tomb of Beaufort and a statue of Joan of Arc erected in 1923.

The shrine of Bishop Gardiner who married Philip of Spain to Mary Tudor is in the north choir aisle, and in the extreme east of the the cathedral the thirteenth-century Lady Chapel, beautified by Henry VII to commemorate the baptism of his eldest son Prince Arthur. North of the Lady Chapel is that of the Guardian Angels, and to the south the Chapel of Bishop Langton.

Winchester Bible

The Library contains the twelfth-century Winchester Bible, the earliest English manuscript still in existence, and a fine collection of printed books bequeathed by George Morley, Bishop of Winchester from 1662 until 1684.

Outside the cathedral, to the west, is the Hampshire and Isle of Wight War Memorial, and another to the King's Royal Rifle Corps.

The ruins of the Chapter House are on the east of the Close, as is the Prior's Lodging, now the Deanery: this is where Philip of Spain lodged before his marriage to Mary Tudor.

Dome Alley nearby has attractive seventeenth-century houses, and Cheyney Court, south of the Deanery, boasts a fine timber-framed house. To the west of the Close is St. Thomas' Church, and the extensive barracks. On the south of it you will see King's Gate and St. Swithin's Church. Immediately to the south is College Street, where Jane Austen lived.

The College

Winchester College buildings lie to the south of College Street. These are open to the public on weekdays and on Sunday afternoons, when official tours are available. St. Mary's College, as it is officially called, was founded by William of Wykeham in 1382. It is built around two quadrangles, the Refectory and Chapel adjoining the inner one. Field Marshal Lord Wavell, soldier-poet and Viceroy of India, lies buried in the Cloister, in the centre of which is the Chantry Chapel where the east window contains the oldest known picture of William of Wykeham. To the south of the quadrangles is a detached building known as 'School', which was built in 1683.

Wolvesey Castle

In College Street, east of the cathedral, is the twelfth-century Wolvesey Castle where Philip of Spain and Mary I of England spent part of their unhappy honeymoon.

The castle was demolished by Cromwell; nearby Wren built an episcopal palace in 1684, and the Bishop of Winchester now resides in the surviving wing.

A mile south of Winchester, and best reached by walking along the bank of the River Itchen, lies the Hospital of St. Cross which houses 25 old men. Founded in 1136 by Bishop Henry de Blois, half brother of King Stephen, it is one of the oldest charitable institutions in the country.

Other Old Buildings

Winchester has a fine selection of interesting old buildings, probably the most impressive being God Begot's House, and that occupied by Lloyds Bank in the High Street, where there are also others worth seeing.

The churches of St. John the Baptist in St. John's Street and St. Bartholomew Hyde in King Alfred's Place off Hyde Street are the most interesting.

View-points

St. Giles Hill to the east of the city has a view-finder in the park at the top, while St. Catherine's Hill over a mile to the south should be visited on account of the prehistoric camp, site of the first settlement, and also for the view over the Itchen Valley.

ROMSEY

Population: 10,000
Early Closing Day: Wednesday

ROMSEY IS A SMALL TOWN on the River Test, eleven miles south-west of Winchester and sixteen south-east of Salisbury. It is dominated by its Abbey Church, but the centre is the Market Place where stands the statue of Romsey's most famous son, Lord Palmerston (1784–1865), the mid-Victorian Prime Minister.

Around the Market Place there are several old coaching inns which point to the importance of Romsey in times past, as a stopping place between Salisbury and Southampton. The White Horse hotel is interesting on account of its mummers' gallery and sixteenth-century wall paintings.

Romsey Abbey

On the right of the Town Hall is a road leading to Romsey Abbey. This approach gives an excellent view of the building, one of Britain's foremost examples of Norman architecture. The Abbey was founded by Edward the Elder, son of Alfred the Great, as a Benedictine monastery: the present building was its church.

The first Abbess was Elfleda, daughter of Edward the Elder. Edmund the Atheling died here in 972 and in 1000 the first church was destroyed in a Danish raid, and was rebuilt in stone.

After the Dissolution of the Monasteries, the abbey church was sold to the Crown by the townsfolk for £100.

Romsey Abbey is cruciform in shape, with a squat tower surmounted by a smaller one. It remains almost untouched since 1130, the year in which it was completed. The choir is square-ended and there are north and south aisles in both the nave and the choir. An extra north transept, which was added for the use of the townspeople in the days of the monastery was pulled down at the Dissolution.

There are north and south transepts and an ambulatory, a passage behind the altar connecting the north and south choir transepts.

Saxon Rood

The north transept contains a lovely sixteenth-century painted reredos. The clerestory of the nave is interesting because of the change of style from Norman in the east, through Transitional, to Early English in the west. The Chapel of St. Anne at the east end of the south choir aisle contains an interesting rood, or crucifix, dating from Saxon times: there is another famous rood on the outside west wall of the transept, which was once part of the cloister.

The Abbey is unusual in having no west door: this is because persons other than monks were not allowed in this part of the church.

Hunting Lodge

Near the Abbey is King John's Hunting Lodge, an ancient house rediscovered in the twentieth century and given to the town in 1946: it now contains a small museum.

There is a fine Tudor house in Palmerston Street known as the Old Manor House. Embley Park School, two miles west of Romsey on the Salisbury road was the home of Florence Nightingale: she lies buried at East Wellow, a mile to the west.

MOTTISFONT ABBEY

About four and a half miles to the north-west of Romsey, in
the delightful valley of the River Test, stands Mottisfont Abbey,
once an Augustinian Priory—although little remains of the
twelfth-century structure. Most of the present building dates from
the eighteenth-century building, or later. The interior is noted for
the splendid drawing-room designed by Rex Whistler: in the
extensive grounds there are fine lawns, specimen trees and water
gardens of some charm, a most enjoyable place to visit, especially
in sunny weather.

AROUND WINCHESTER

In the vicinity of Winchester there are many other places worth
visiting, and excursions about the countryside can embrace several
features in one journey, although many are lovely and interesting
enough to warrant spending a whole day in the one place.

Marwell Zoological Park is at Fishers Pond, about six miles south
from Winchester. It is in the 250-acre setting of the grounds of
Marwell Hall, and has a considerable collection of animals some of
them very rare, in spacious enclosures. One may either walk or drive
in a car to see the animals.

Bishops Waltham is a small town with an ancient centre, around
which modern suburbs have developed. Here there are extensive
ruins of a palace built by Henry de Blois in 1136 for the use of the
Bishops of Winchester. William Wykeham made additions in the
fifteenth century, but Cromwell damaged the place very severely.

St. Peter's Church has a fine Jacobean pulpit. In the Crown Hotel
there is a collection of arms and armour.

Old Winchester Hill

South-east from Winchester lies the lovely valley of the River
Meon, and Carhampton with its largely Saxon church where there
are many interesting features including wall paintings, an ancient
altar, and a stone coffin. The inevitable huge and ancient yew tree
dominates the churchyard.

Just to the east, Old Winchester Hill, 653 feet in height and with
remains of an ancient camp, affords splendid views over the Meon
Valley.

There is a Nature Trail.

Link with Cromwell

The attractive village of Hursley is situated about five miles
south-west of Winchester on the main road to Romsey. It has some
old and pretty cottages, and the Church of All Saints, rebuilt by
John Keble, which contains a monument to Oliver Cromwell's son
Richard. There are interesting Cromwellian records in the church
register.

Farley Mount

Due west from Winchester, at a distance of about five miles and charmingly situated on Pitt Down, is Farley Mount, a splendid downland area, affording many views over the surrounding countryside. This is an ideal walking area, though it is equally delightful just to sit and enjoy the views. A monument on a hill-top commemorates a prodigious leap once made by horse and rider where both survived unscathed.

Attractive Village

About five miles north-west of Winchester is the attractive village of Crawley, set well away from the main road, and amid rolling downlands. Here too are many delightful old-world timbered cottages and a church dating from Norman times, with additions from later periods.

Avington Park

In the lovely Itchen Valley, about four miles from Winchester to the north-east, lies Avington Park, an eighteenth-century house with a lake, set in extensive parkland. In the grounds there stands a lovely eighteenth-century church built in red brick: it is very striking inside, with box-pews, pulpit, and handsome canopies and reredos. There is a notable Crucifixion window.

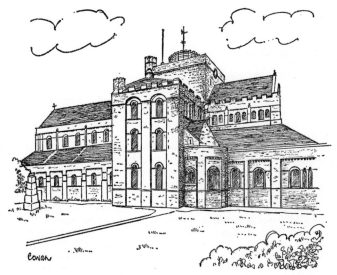

Romsey Abbey, South Front

ALRESFORD

'Old' and 'New' Alresford, divided by a bridge over the River Alre, form an extremely pretty and picturesque country town. An old fulling-mill is a notable relic, as are the fine Georgian houses. Mary Mitford who wrote *Our Village* was born in Broad Street.

In Alresford, too, Mary Sumner founded the Mothers' Union and in the eighteenth-century church of St. Mary in the old town lies Admiral Lord Rodney, one of the heroes of Cape St. Vincent and Trafalgar.

To the west of Old Alresford there is a lovely stretch of downland called Abbotstone Down, overlooking the Itchen Valley and affording some really impressive views far beyond. It is a lovely picnic or walking place, and has an atmosphere of antiquity borne out by the earthwork which shows that our remote ancestors defended it, from the height known as Oliver's Battery.

Tichborne Dole

A little to the south-west of Alresford is the pretty, old-world village of Tichborne. Tichborne Park, seat of the Tichborne family, is the scene of an 800-year-old ceremony which takes place each Lady Day when a quantity of flour is blessed and then distributed among poor people. This is known as the Tichborne Dole.

In the partly Saxon church there are some interesting memorials of the Tichborne family.

PETERSFIELD

Population: 8,750
Early Closing Day: Thursday
Market Days: Wednesday and Saturday

ASTRIDE THE MAIN LONDON to Portsmouth road is Petersfield, an old market town with a handsome square dominated by an equestrian statue of William III in Roman dress—a favourite style with sculptors when representing royalty.

The restored Norman church retains much of the original stonework while near the Square, and in College, and Dragon Streets, fine old houses abound: some are handsomely timbered and some have overhanging upper storeys. On the heath or common, there is a lovely tree-lined lake.

A short distince due north lies Steep, a beauty spot in the hills, and amid glorious woodlands. Here there is a lovely old church still with much of the Norman work to be seen. It contains a wonderful silver chalice, complete with cover. Here, too, there is the massive yew tree which was so much a feature of ancient churchyards.

Westward from Steep is Stoner Hill, a lofty view-point from which there are fine vistas over the surrounding country.

Buriton

Just east of the A3, about three miles south from Petersfield, is the village of Buriton with lofty Butser Hill dominating the western skyline.

The little church is Norman and Early English, with fine stonework and wood carving, as well as traces of wall paintings which are at least six hundred years old.

In the Georgian Manor House, the historian Edward Gibbon spent his boyhood. He was the author of the great *Decline and Fall of the Roman Empire*, one of the most notable historical works ever written.

Mass Dial

About four miles west of Buriton, nestling among country lanes, is East Meon, a charming old-world village, set in the Meon Valley and below the glorious downs.

The church is Norman and Early English, has a mass dial, and a magnificent, highly decorated font of black Tournai marble.

The old Manor House nearby was once the Court House of the Bishops of Winchester.

Queen Elizabeth Country Park

This joint venture of the Hampshire County Council and the Forestry Commission was opened by Her Majesty the Queen in 1976. It extends over 1,400 acres of lovely countryside including War Down, Holt Down, and Butser Hill – 888 feet. The Park Centre houses exhibitions, displays and informative material. There is a theatre where tape-and-slide shows about the Park can be seen, Forest Walks and a Forest Drive: many other activities are available. Refreshments can be obtained and there are ample parking facilities. Access to the Park is directly from the A3, two miles south of Petersfield.

ALTON

Population: 12,700
Early Closing Day: Wednesday
Market Day: Tuesday

SITUATED ABOUT SEVENTEEN MILES north-east of Winchester on the A31 road from Guildford, Alton is an historic market town on the old route known as the Pilgrim's Way which led from Winchester, across Hampshire, Surrey and Kent to the 'Golden Shrine' of St. Thomas à Becket at Canterbury.

The splendid church is mainly fifteenth-century, though its foundation was in the twelfth. The tower contains some of the original Norman work as do some of the windows. The font is Norman, and there is some very fine wood carving. There are some interesting bullet marks on doors and pillars, especially the south door, which bear testimony to a story of heroic resistance during the Civil War by a party of Royalists under Colonel Boles who, with a small group of infantry, strove to hold Alton against a much superior Roundead force. Colonel Boles was gradually driven back into the church were he was shot down in the pulpit. There is a notable cross and brass commemorating this brave colonel who defended, so stubbornly, the Stuart cause.

Edmund Spenser

There is still to be found, in Amery Street, an ancient cottage which was for a short time the home of Edmund Spenser. This great and gifted poet was one of the pioneers of the resurgence of English poetry, and is remembered mainly for his pastoral *The Shepheard's Calendar*, the six books of the *Faerie Queen* and for his sonnets which rank between those of Sidney and Shakespeare.

It was Spenser who first paid tribute to the 'father of English literature' Geoffrey Chaucer, and coined the famous expression in which he described the author of *The Canterbury Tales* as a 'well of English, pure and undefiled'.

The Curtis Museum

Open to the public on weekdays, this museum houses a remarkable collection of old farming implements and other items of agricultural interest, as well as many antiquities relating to the town and surrounding countryside: some date back to Roman times.

Alton also has a seventeenth-century Grammar School, and some pleasant old Almshouses.

CHAWTON

About a mile-and-a-half to the south-west of Alton is Chawton, just off the main A31. The village is famous as the last home of Jane Austen, the writer whose immortal works have given so many 'characters' to English literature. She was Hampshire-born (at Steventon near Basingstoke), and apart from visits to London and Bath, spent most of her life in her native county.

At Chawton she settled in with her brother Edward and his household, and there wrote *Emma* and *Persuasion*. Her most famous story, *Pride and Prejudice*, is world-famous, but many 'Austenites' consider *Emma* to be just as artistically perfect, and possibly, a greater book.

Jane herself is buried in Winchester Cathedral, but her last home in Chawton is now a Museum operated by the Jane Austen Memorial Trust. It contains many charming personal relics of Jane and of her family, and is open daily, including Bank Holidays.

The house is a substantial-looking red-brick edifice, and that, and the grounds may well have been the model for the home of Emma Woodhouse in the novel *Emma*.

The church at Chawton is modern, the older one having been destroyed by fire, but it is an attractive place with an unexpected charm.

SELBORNE

Almost due south of Alton, some four and a half miles along the B3006, is the quiet attractive village of Selborne, and 'The Wakes', immortalised by its famous naturalist-Rector, Gilbert White, in his celebrated *Natural History of Selborne*.

Gilbert White was a peace-loving scholarly observer of nature, born at the house in Selborne, and leaving only to take Holy Orders—which he did between 1747 and 1751. Thereafter he retired to 'The Wakes', and by means of his Diary and his letters to friends, compiled an enchanting record of rural life in the eighteenth century and added enormously to the sum of knowledge of the birds and animals of the English countryside.

This is one of the few places which are still recognisable as described by White. There are the same stretches of common land as well as the thirty acres of 'The Wakes' estate, between the village of Selborne and Selborne Hill, given to the National Trust by Magdalen College Oxford in 1932. Other areas have been added to the Trust, including the 'Great Hanger'—the stretch of hanging beech woods so often mentioned in White's book.

Oates Museum

A later tenant of 'The Wakes' was Captain Laurence Oates, the 'very gallant gentleman' who died on Scott's tragic Antarctic journey. One of the rooms in 'The Wakes' is an Oates Museum, with relics of the man who walked out alone into the blizzard to die when he feared that his companions might lose their own chance of survival through consideration for him, when illness slowed him down in the march back to base. Among the other personal items connected with Oates, in this modern wing of the place, there is a sledge used in the expedition to the South Pole.

The lovely old seventeenth-century house is set in gardens designed by Gilbert White himself, and the author of one of the most scholarly, yet readable, great works of Natural History, lies in the pretty churchyard which is presided over by another of those massive yew trees so loved by our forebears.

The beautiful old church has a Gilbert White Memorial Window.

Hawksley Hanger

Set among hills and woods of great beauty, about two miles south of Selborne, is Empshott. Here the little church dates from the

H

twelfth century although there has been rebuilding in later periods: there is some fine wood carving to be seen.

Hawksley Hanger, a mile further south, is a beautifully wooded hill often described in Gilbert White's *Natural History*. It affords excellent panoramic views over the country around.

BRAMSHOTT

In the extreme south-east corner of Hampshire, beyond the area of Bordon Military camp there is a charming region of woodlands and hills, with open common lands, much of which is in the care of the National Trust.

The village of Bramshott is in a beautiful setting with pinewoods and hills, and has many old and attractive buildings. The old church, thirteenth-century in origin, has been much rebuilt and renovated, and is most attractively situated among yew trees.

To the east of the village lies Bramshott Chase, commonland in close proximity to the Portsmouth road.

North of the village, and among more lovely woodland is the chain of small ponds known as Waggoners' Wells, formed originally as fish ponds. One of these was, in fact, a hammer pond at one time, serving a long-vanished iron works. This area is always accessible, being National Trust property, and a popular beauty spot, as also is Ludshott Common nearby.

BENTWORTH

Some three miles west of Alton, among lovely downs, is the small village of Bentworth where the ancient church has many interesting features, some of which date back to the twelfth century. The priest's doorway and the west window are very old indeed, as is the font. There is some notably attractive woodwork.

Godsfield Chapel

About four miles south-west from Bentworth, close by a farm, stands a small building erected originally for the Knights of St. John in the fourteenth century. There are just two little rooms and a chapel, making an interesting link with medieval history: the Knights of St. John were suppressed when they ceased to keep vows of poverty and chastity and sought to become an altogether more worldly political power.

BINSTED

North-east out of Alton, via Holybourne where there is an attractive Norman church with good carving and interesting windows, a country lane bears due eastwards, at Cuckoo's Corner, to Binsted about four miles away.

This pretty village looks out over hop-growing country, and stands on the site of ancient earlier settlements. It was known to the Romans who left traces for later generations to uncover, while the Normans bequeathed to the future the charming church. There is also some particularly fine Jacobean woodwork to be seen there, and a handsome effigy of a knight in armour which dates from the fourteenth century.

Immediately north of Binsted, over the main Farnham road, is Froyle. Here the eighteenth-century church has many much older features incorporated in its structure, including a fourteenth-century chancel, and a very lovely east window. There are some other handsome windows and two fine chalices.

Lord Baden-Powell

Two miles beyond Froyle, along the A31, is Bentley, at one time the home of Lord Baden-Powell, the famous defender of Mafeking during the South African War, and later founder of the world-wide Boy Scout Movement with its famous motto 'Be Prepared'. Later he founded a kindred movement, the Girl Guides, so that not only boys, but also their sisters might be drawn into similar groups where the aims were to give them honourable and patriotic ideas of service to their country and to the world.

Lord Baden-Powell presented to the village its 'sign' which is a 'book' carved in stone which gives details of the area.

The old churchyard has some fine yew trees, and behind the Norman church there is a splendid avenue of beech trees. Inside the church there is a good Norman font.

To the south-east, across the A31, and south of the River Wey, is the attractive Alice Holt Forest, which has a road through it, and is accessible to the public.

ALDERSHOT

Population: 33,900
Early Closing Day: Wednesday

THIS FAMOUS GARRISON TOWN, often called 'Soldiers Town', has long been an important military centre—the 'home' of the British Army. The smart, clean and tidy 'lines' (barracks and other military establishments), reflect great credit on British military men. Here too, is the Army Sports Centre, a fine stadium where athletic and team events are held annually.

Heroes' Shrine

The Heroes' Shrine on Church Hill was designed as a rockery, made from material collected in 54 bombed boroughs. The Royal

Garrison Church of All Saints, with its 121-feet tower, is set in a most attractive place on Claycart Road. It displays many Regimental Colours and houses also a great many memorials to those who fell in war. Near this church is the huge equestrian statue of the Duke of Wellington, designed by Matthew Wyatt, which once crowned the Wellington Arch at the top of Constitution Hill in London. It was removed and brought to Aldershot in 1883, when road widening was in progress in the capital.

Other Churches

The Garrison Church of St. George is noted for its modern stained glass windows, while St. Michael's the parish church has a fifteenth-century tower and some interesting old monuments.

Museums

Among places of special interest are the various museums in Aldershot. That of the Airborne Forces has a good collection of special equipment used by the Airborne Troops. The Royal Army Medical Corps Museum contains uniforms, flags, medals, letters and relics of Miss Florence Nightingale and also of Lt. Col. Martin Leake, twice winner of the Victoria Cross, the only man to have done so. The Museum of the Royal Army Dental Corps contains some instruments which indicate the immense improvement in Army dental care since the days of the First Expeditionary Force of 1914.

Earthworks

About a mile to the south-west of the town is an ancient earthwork called Caesar's Camp, and there is another just north of the Wellington Monument.

FARNBOROUGH

Though almost a northern extension of Aldershot, Farnborough strives to develop a separate business and domestic character. In close proximity there are several military camps and the Royal Aircraft Establishment, under whose aegis the great Farnborough Air Show takes place biennially.

Situated in the north of Farnborough is Farnborough Hill, the home of the Empress Eugénie of France when she was in exile. After she moved from her first home in exile, at Chislehurst, Kent, the Empress had the body of her husband, Napoleon III, exhumed and re-interred in the Roman Catholic church belonging to the Benedictine Abbey which she founded. The body of her son, the Prince Imperial who was killed fighting with the British during the Zulu War, is also buried there, and when the Empress died in 1920 she too was interred in the royal mausoleum.

Today, Farnborough Hill, a nineteenth-century mansion is a public school for girls. The parish church dates from the twelfth century and has much Norman work still intact. There are some remarkable ancient wall-paintings and some splendid Jacobean woodwork.

FLEET

Just four miles north-west of Aldershot is Fleet, a growing residential locality, pleasantly situated amid open common land. North of the town is Fleet Pond, a lake of some 130 acres, and once an ecclesiastical supply depot—for the monks of Winchester used to fish here! In the nineteenth-century red brick church are some marble figures set under a decorated canopy.

Ancient Brass

A similar distance south-west of Aldershot is the old and charming village of Crondall where there is a fine old timbered inn. A splendid avenue of lime trees leads to the large Norman church with its seventeenth-century red brick tower. In the interior the chancel has a vaulted roof and there is much other Norman work as well as a brass portrait of great age, claimed to be the very oldest in Hampshire. Besides other brasses there is a Norman font, another in marble and a magnificent chest, about 6,000 years old.

YATELEY

About five miles to the north-west of Farnborough, beyond the pines and heaths of Blackwater, is the ancient village of Yateley. Here is an Early English church displaying much Norman detail. A more modern item of considerable beauty is the east window by Burne-Jones. Among the treasures here are some good Crosses, and a unique crystal cup dating from 1675, which are very beautiful and valuable adornments to the church. The lych-gate dates from 1625.

Charles Kingsley

On the Berkshire border, about two miles north-west of Yateley, is Eversley where Charles Kingsley was first curate and later vicar. Here much of his literary work was undertaken, in between teaching at the school. His range was remarkable for he was a poet, essayist, historical novelist and romantic writer as well as an established Church of England clergyman. Indeed he became a Canon of Westminster and Chaplain to Queen Victoria.

Yet this 'pillar of the Establishment' was possessed of broad sympathies and depth of understanding far beyond his own social and ecclesiastical world, as is proved by his books *Alton Locke* and *Yeast* which virtually forecast the rise of the Socialist movement, while the immortal *Water Babies* showed his concern for the wretched condition of poor children as symbolised by Tom, the little chimney-sweeper. Of his historical works, *Hypatia* is a brilliant work on the rise of Christianity in ancient Alexandria, and his most famous is *Westward Ho!* a tale of Anglo-Spanish rivalry in Tudor times, on the high seas and in the New World.

The rectory where he lived and worked is close by the church where he sleeps beneath a handsome marble cross. The church dates from the eighteenth century when it was much rebuilt but it contains a fine chancel screen and exceptionally fine Cross from the sixteenth century.

ANDOVER

Population: 26,700
Early Closing Day: Wednesday
Market Day: Saturday

SITUATED IN THE NORTH OF HAMPSHIRE, some fourteen miles north-west of Winchester, Andover is an old agricultural and market town, now fast-developing and encircled by modern roads. Both Saxons and Romans knew this locality and many encampments and burial grounds may be seen on the higher ground surrounding Andover. The mainly nineteenth-century church contains memorials from an earlier church—the Venables tomb being outstanding. There are several fine old inns in the town.

Abbots Ann

This is a lovely little place about two miles south-west of Andover. It has thatched, black and white timbered cottages. In the eighteenth-century church there is a splendid gallery and up high above the nave, two rows of white paper garlands—memorials of young unmarried men and women buried here, who were pure in heart and mind.

Motor Racing Circuit

About four-and-a-half miles west from Andover lies Thruxton which has a church dating from the thirteenth century, with sixteenth-century and later additions. There are several fine monuments within and much excellent wood carving. At Thruxton there is a famous motor-racing circuit.

Wild Life Park

Famous for Weyhill Fair, held annually in October and authorised by a Charter of 1599, Weyhill, four miles west of Andover is an attractive village also noted for its Wild Life Park. The parish church is mainly nineteenth-century, but some portions and certain of the furnishings are much older.

TIDWORTH

Five miles west of Weyhill is Tidworth, a noted military centre of some importance. There are two outstanding annual events at Tidworth—the Military Tattoo and the Three Day Horse Trials. Those interested will look out for these dates around May and June each year.

HURSTBOURNE TARRANT

Five miles due north from Andover and nestling in the narrow valley of the River Test is Hurstbourne Tarrant with much fine woodland and rolling downs in the vicinity. William Cobbett in his *Rural Rides* refers to Hurstbourne Tarrant as 'Uphusband'. Some pretty cottages and a church which contains some twelfth-century work as well as some later building, add character to this delightful village. An exhibition of arts, crafts and sculpture is being developed here with a view to becoming a permanent feature of the place.

HIGHCLERE

Six miles northward out of Hurstbourne Tarrant is Highclere, astride the A343 and amid the rolling downs. Here is a Victorian

Wherwell

Castle, designed by Sir Charles Barry in 1842, and set in a magnificent privately-owned estate, the grounds of which were laid out by 'Capability' Brown. Originally a country home for the Bishops of Winchester, this lovely park is a picture with its lakes and wooded hills, its glorious banks of rhododendrons and azaleas and specimen trees. To the south is Sidown Hill, 872 feet, and westward lies Pilot Hill which is, at 874 feet, a fine viewing point.

Harewood Forest

To the east of Andover is Harewood Forest, a very attractive area of woodland, once part of a great hunting forest. The Romans and Saxons have each left traces here. East of the Forest is the valley of the delightful River Test with a series of lovely villages along the banks. Starting south of Andover and proceeding in a north-easterly direction one comes to Chilbolton with a parish church worth seeing. Dating originally from the twelfth century it has a fourteenth-century screen and a handsome pulpit. Near here is West Down, another splendid view-point.

At the junction of the B3420 with the B3048, stands Wherwell, a pretty thatched village with a nineteenth-century church. According to an inscription upon a wall, an Abbey was once sited here. The inn at Wherwell is the 'Twentieth Century'. About three miles further along the same route is Longparish, also with thatched cottages, and a lovely thirteenth-century parish church. In the church there is a rare hour-glass and a notable, tall font-cover. Where the B3048 is crossed by the B3400, stands Hurstbourne Priors; here the church, though much rebuilt still contains some of the original Norman structure. Here there is a rare 'Mass Clock' on the wall, and among the memorials, the canopied tomb of Sir Robert Oxenbridge. Beside the A34, just south of Whitchurch is the village of Tufton where there is also a lovely old church, dating back to Norman times but with later additions. It has a remarkable wall painting which is very ancient, and other interesting items in the interior. The general setting is very pretty.

BASINGSTOKE

Population: 59,110
Early Closing Day: Thursday
Market Days: Wednesday/Saturday

ONCE A SMALL COUNTRY MARKET TOWN, Basingstoke is now a fast-growing and busy industrial centre surrounded by new suburban residential estates. This is because the ubiquitous motor-car and the motor-roads built to accommodate it have made this kind of new development around old towns a practical and viable proposition.

The M3 and M4 motorways, together with regular train services means that London may be reached quickly, either by private or public transport, and similarly with the Midland regions, or the great port of Southampton, which is only thirty miles away to the south.

Basingstoke now has large engineering works, and there is a thriving clothing manufacturing industry, also printing works, while the town still retains its important links with agriculture, farming, and nursery gardens. The new pedestrian precinct covers some twelve acres of ground between New Market Square and the bus station. Being set in a naturally 'bowl-shaped' area, the precinct has been landscaped and terraced at various levels which gives it an especially attractive appearance.

The shops themselves are serviced from roads constructed underneath the pedestrian paths, whilst parking for thousands of cars is available above the shops, and leading to the high-level access roads. The precinct affords many unexpected and attractive viewing points from its galleries and steps, and there is ample provision for seating.

As well as the well-known multiple stores there are also some smaller, more personal little shops still to be found.

Holy Ghost Chapel

Off Chapel Hill, just north of the railway station, is an ancient burial ground in which stand the ruins of the thirteenth-century Chapel of the Holy Ghost. This part was, in fact, really Holy Trinity Chantry which was added to the original Chapel of the Holy Ghost in 1542. The earlier chapel was the mortuary chapel of an extra-mural burial ground used during the period between 1208 to 1214 when King John and his whole kingdom were under an interdict from the Pope of Rome. Of this building only the part of a wall and the adjacent west tower remain, the rest being, as has been said, the ruins of the added chantry.

Parish Church

The church of St. Michael and All Angels is now mainly a sixteenth-century structure with some traces of the earlier Norman building. The two-storey porch dates from 1539. The mainly Perpendicular style building is noted for a fearsome array of gargoyles which gaze down from the tower, and there is a very handsome interior with a fine screen, altar, an old font, and a very ancient alms-box. Other features of interest include the Corporation Pew, a library of Puritan theological works, and a Memorial Chapel reredos which is a tryptich, painted in 1549, and believed to be the work of a pupil of Leonardo da Vinci. There is also an eighteenth-century monument to Thomas Warton whose sons became, one Poet Laureate, and the other headmaster of Winchester College. The emblem of the church depicting St. Michael slaying a dragon is also the official emblem of Basingstoke.

The town had always been a Saxon royal manor and in A.D. 945 was granted to the Queen Edgira and her heirs, a gift which was confirmed by the Domesday Survey of 1085. In Norman times the place grew gradually in importance and by 1214 had a market charter. This market was held every Wednesday down the centuries until comparatively recent times. Today that cattle market has been replaced by general markets on Wednesdays and Saturdays.

Ancient Charters

Basingstoke collected various charters from the hands of successive monarchs but although these documents have been lost they are recorded safely enough. However, the civic authorities do possess two later charters, one from James I and the other from Charles I. The coaching roads, canals, and finally the railway services helped in the building up of the former village into an agricultural centre, a cloth-making town and today into a busy, humming commercial centre housing many and varied enterprises. Now, the green countryside which once opened up each side of the railway is the heart of the modern factory and housing developments which have so transformed Basingstoke.

Another reminder of the more gracious past exists in the seventeenth-century Deanes Almshouses which are of interest, while the War Memorial Park between the London Road and the by-pass is a pleasant oasis in this very bustling community.

THE VYNE

Less than three miles north-west of Basingstoke is the village of Sherborne St. John where the Perpendicular church has fine old monuments and brasses, a Norman font and a chained library. About a mile to the north-east is a fine Tudor manor house known as The Vyne, built by Lord Sandys and later extended by John Webb.

The interior panelling is the work of superb Tudor craftsmen, and an ornamental staircase, built in the eighteenth century, is magnificent. Most beautiful of all, perhaps, is the private Chapel where the tiling, carving, and Flemish glasswork are outstanding.

Among the many illustrious visitors to this place were Henry VIII and his daughter, Elizabeth I.

Today The Vyne is in the care of the National Trust and is open to the public in summer on Wednesdays and Bank Holidays. It is also open, in the afternoons only, during summer on Thursdays and Sundays.

Rare Effigy

Journeying two miles further from Sherborne St. John one reaches the village of Pamber. Here a fine avenue of oak trees leads to the ancient church, once part of a Benedictine Priory dating from A.D. 1110. The Norman tower of this most lovely building has been restored carefully and there are many interesting features in the interior. There are some good murals, a panelled font and a rare wooden effigy of a knight with chain mail and a surcoat.

Link with Canterbury

Due north from Basingstoke at a distance of about five miles, is the pretty village of Bramley with its thatched cottages and Tudor manor house. The little church of St. James is fascinating, dating from Norman times, with considerable later building. It has a series of wall-paintings, one of which depitcs in detail the murder of Thomas à Becket in Canterbury Cathedral. The window glass is especially beautiful, particularly the Brocas Chapel where the south window is really lovely. The marble tomb in this chapel is of eighteenth-century workmanship, not established, though often attributed to Banks.

SILCHESTER

Two miles north of Bramley is the village of Silchester which was the site of the grand Roman city of Calleva Atrebatum. Much of the original wall is still to be seen, especially near the church, where the remains are about one-and-a-half miles in length, and twelve feet high: but the rest of Calleva lies hidden beneath the meadows inside the former walls. Excavations revealed the complete ground plan of the original city and confirmed, as always, the wonderful standards of building which characterised those formidable empire-builders. There was, in fact, a city in existence before they arrived, but it was the Romans who gave the place the stamp of their own grandeur of conception and practice.

Classical Buildings

Through four gates in the walls one could enter Roman Calleva Atrebatum and find oneself in a community of fine, classical buildings, spacious piazzas or squares, and large houses. The places of public assembly were even more spacious and grand and the sites of the Forum, Temple Basilica and the Baths have all been carefully traced and recorded. There was even a Christian church.

Museums

Reading Museum now houses the more important discoveries of Calleva, but there is also a small local museum, opened in 1951. The village church, St. Mary's, is medieval and has an eighteenth-century pulpit, a fourteenth-century font and a fifteenth-century screen.

Portway

A mile to the west of Silchester is a Roman milestone, and the line of the track known as Portway, linking Calleva with Old Sarum (Salisbury), may still be traced.

KINGSCLERE

In a splendid setting amid the chalk downs, south-west from
Silchester and some eight-and-a-half miles north-westwards from
Basingstoke, lies the old market town of Kingsclere. The church is
mainly Norman though much rebuilt, and contains a handsome
seventeenth-century carved pulpit, brass candelabra, and silver
chalices. The famous monument of the Kingsmills is in alabaster.

To the south lies Cottington's Hill, a really splendid viewing-point
capped with ancient earthworks. Two miles to the east is the village
of Wolverton where there is a lovely eighteenth-century red-brick
church with much fine carved oak furnishing.

Paper-mills

In the lovely Test Valley, some nine miles west of Basingstoke,
is Laverstoke where, since the eighteenth century the paper-mills
have made the paper for Bank of England notes.

The large, modern church contains a magnificent reredos and a
very beautiful screen.

Two miles west of Laverstoke is Whitchurch, an old market town
with an ancient Town Hall. In the restored church there is an inscribed
Anglo-Saxon burial stone, a fifteenth-century font, and some
interesting brasses.

DUMMER

Situated just off the M3, about five miles south-west of
Basingstoke, Dummer is a very ancient village with roots in
pre-history, but deriving its name from a distinguished local family.
The Early English and Perpendicular church attracts visitors bent on
seeing the unusual fifteenth-century wooded canopy above the
chancel arch and also the fourteenth-century pulpit. This is where
George Whitefield preached when he was a curate. There are some
good brasses and a fine fifteenth-century gallery.

The manor house near the church dates from the eighteenth
century.

Jane Austen

About three miles to the north-west of Dummer, across the
motorway, lies Steventon, birthplace of the famous novelist Jane
Austen. Her birth in 1775 is commemorated in the church where her
father was the vicar. The old manorial pew is still to be seen there.

BASING

Just to the north-east of Basingstoke, at a distance of roughly
two miles, is the village of Basing which earned a place in history
during the English Civil War. The sixteenth-century manor house
here withstood a siege by the Roundheads for two years, the

Royalists surrendering finally only when Cromwell himself undertook the storming of the place. Among the prisoners he captured was Inigo Jones the architect. Today only the ruins of old Basing House are to be seen, but among these the gate-house, tithe-barn and dovecote are interesting.

The church, St. Mary's, dates originally from Norman times but has a good deal of much later period work in it. The font dates from the fifteenth century and there are handsome, sculptured tombs of the Paulet family.

Not far away, about two miles westward, is Nateley Scures, where there is a small Norman church displaying a mermaid carved above the doorway. Inside there are some curious epitaphs.

Ancient Water-Mill
The River Loddon runs northwards near Basing, and crosses the A33 at Sherfield on Loddon three miles to the north. This is a picturesque little place with old houses, and an ancient water-mill set around the pretty village green.

The church has been much rebuilt but has an ancient history, and there are some interesting old brasses.

STRATFIELD SAYE
Just two miles northward from Sherfield is Stratfield Saye, a small village fringing a huge estate of the same name. Built originally in the reign of Charles I, the house was presented in 1817 to Arthur Wellesley, first Duke of Wellington, by a grateful nation after he had destroyed forever the Napoleonic threat to Britain's security by his victory at Waterloo in 1815, and by his settlement of European affairs afterwards.

Wellington's Charger
The house and Pleasure Grounds are now open to the public between Easter and mid-September, every day except Tuesday, between 11·30 a.m. and 5·30 p.m. The house contains a unique collection of paintings, furniture, effects and particular relics of the 'Great Duke', the most celebrated soldier-statesman of his age.

Not far away from the house is the grave of Copenhagen, the Duke's favourite charger, the horse which carried him all day at Waterloo.

Country Park
In another part of the Stratfield Saye estate, a delightful stretch of woodland has been made into a country park. Here there are nature trails, camping sites, and a charming lake which offers attractions for both boaters and fishermen. Waterloo Meadow is an attractive picnic site, or alternatively there is a cafeteria at hand. Car parking is free.

ODIHAM

The old market town of Odiham lies on the A287 near its junction with the A32, about six miles east of Basingstoke. The broad and ancient main street is lined with handsome Georgian houses and the Early English church is approached through a glorious avenue of lime trees; this has a very interesting interior containing a magnificent seventeenth-century carved pulpit, fifteenth-century screens, carved galleries, a seven-hundred-year-old piscina and some ancient brasses.

By the wall of the churchyard are the old stocks and whipping-post: an even more remarkable survival is the Pest House, dating from the Plague Years.

There are some seventeenth-century almshouses nearby.

Odiham Castle

There is a most attractive gabled vicarage which dates from Tudor times and has some seventeenth-century additions, whilst on the other side of it are some picturesque old cottages.

To the north-west, barely a mile distant, is all that remains of Odiham Castle. There is only the shell of the Keep, but it is still a fascinating relic of the place from which King John set out for Runnymede and the confrontation with his Barons which ended with the signing of Magna Carta in 1215.

HARTLEY WINTNEY

Astride the main A30, some seven miles east of Basingstoke, set amid pleasant pine woods and open common land is the village of Hartley Wintney. There is a modern church of Victorian origin which is attractive, but the older church, just outside the village, is more picturesque. Part of its structure dates from the fourteenth century, and there is later work also.

Monastic Barn

On Wintney Moor where there was once a Priory there remains now a huge monastic barn and some other ancient outbuildings. A mile to the west of the village is West Green House, standing in seventy-seven acres of ground, most of which is agricultural land. This was once the home of General Hawley who lost a battle to Charles Stuart at Falkirk, but got his revenge at Culloden Moor in April 1746.

Katherine of Aragon

This house was given to the National Trust by Sir Victor Sassoon. At Winchfield, two miles to the south-east is a splendid Norman church with a superbly ornamented interior, while a mile further south-west is Dogmersfield which has associations with Katherine of Aragon, first wife of Henry VIII.